ST. LAWRENCE COUNTY IN THE WAR OF 1812

ST. LAWRENCE COUNTY IN THE WAR OF 1812

FOLLY AND MISCHIEF

JOHN M. AUSTIN

THE History PRESS

Published by The History Press
Charleston, SC 29403
www.historypress.net

First published 2013

Manufactured in the United States

ISBN 978.1.62619.148.8

Library of Congress CIP data applied for.

This book is dedicated to all the citizen-soldiers from St. Lawrence County, New York, who served their country during the War of 1812—and especially to those who lost their lives in that service.

CONTENTS

ACKNOWLEDGEMENTS

The only drawback to making a list of people who assisted with this book is the fear that someone might be inadvertently overlooked. However, a debt is owed to all the following people and perhaps a few others.

The St. Lawrence County Historical Association in Canton provided assistance with some of the maps and illustrations and other resources, including its cemetery inventories. Another huge help was the staff at the St. Lawrence University Library and Archives. The interlibrary loan department cheerfully chased books and newspaper microfilm for me even when I was unsure if they actually existed. Tish Munt was again very valuable in showing me how to save PDF files using the university computers. A huge part of this project was based on the Parish-Rosseel Collection at SLU, and Mark McMurray and Paul Haggett were very gracious in helping me search those records. Christine Zimmerman of SLU also provided translations of some very difficult German letters in that collection.

Bryan Thompson, the DeKalb Historian, inspired me to search some sources at the New York State Archives that I had not thought of and allowed me to use copies of some of the muster rolls and records that he had found. He also provided hints at other resources that turned out to be very handy.

Jim Folts at the New York State Archives was very helpful in my search for court records dating back two hundred years, and the organization was very generous in awarding me a research stipend through the Hackman grant. Wayne Miller, director of the Ogdensburg Public Library, was especially accommodating, letting me spend time in the archives vault searching through the Hasbrouck Collection and other sources and also helping me with some of the scanning. Brigitte Clark and John and Susan Omohundro provided some much-appreciated editing and proofreading, while Roger Baines was very generous with his time and expertise in helping to edit some of the maps and illustrations.

Chapter 1

THE EMPEROR FORD

Nathan Ford was the eighth child of John Ford and Martha Raynor, born in Morristown, New Jersey, on December 8, 1763. His parents died when he was quite young, and he grew up in the home of his Ford grandparents. His early life is not well documented, but his family was apparently quite well off, and it seems likely that he read law in the office of one of the prominent lawyers of the area, perhaps one of the Ogdens. He served as a quartermaster in the Revolution and was obviously a very organized and driven sort of individual. In 1794, he was one of the directors of the Morris Academy in Morristown, and in some way or another (perhaps at court or at some social function), Nathan Ford became acquainted with the Ogden family about this time and apparently drew the attention of Samuel Ogden, a prominent lawyer.

In 1795, Ford took the job of Samuel Ogden's land agent and set himself up in the recently abandoned British fort on the west bank of the Oswegatchie. From that time until the formation of the county, Ford acted as principal developer of the region and worked hard to make roads and other improvements that would help entice settlers to the new territory. He was responsible for the laying out of the Ogdensburg village and selling the first village lots.

Nathan Ford was a staunch Federalist in an age when that party was in decline in most of the United States but still had pockets of control in the northeast, and St. Lawrence County was one of the most Federalist in its views. Federalists were conservatives who believed in a strong federal government and feared the actions of the illiterate mob that might lessen their authority. Federalists tended to be aristocratic moneyed men, Episcopalians in general,[1] who thought that the promotion of private enterprise was the highest possible order. They believed in a more-or-less paternalistic society in which rich, educated men could make decisions for the whole country. They tended to favor relations with the monarchical Great Britain and had nothing but fear and loathing for the democratic rabble that had toppled the French regime in 1789. One of their favorite insults during the War of 1812 was to call a political enemy a "Jacobin," a reference to the grassroots Democratic rebels in France, including Napoleon. Their opponents on the national scene were the Anti-Federalists, or Democratic-Republicans, so any reference in contemporary newspapers to "republican policies" or "democratic maneuvers" referred to those in opposition to the Federalists.[2] The manufacturing centers in the northeast relied on trade and big businesses, so they were naturally the last strongholds of the Federalists and were the most vehement in their opposition to the War of 1812. The Democratic-Republicans held sway in all the southern and western parts of the country and tended to favor individual freedoms and states' rights over that of a strong national government. Farmers, immigrants and common laborers were more likely to be of the Democratic-Republican camp than the Federalist and were far more likely to support the war. The reason the Federalists in New York gained something of a resurgence had more to do with the fact that the only thing the New York Republicans liked better than fighting the Federalists was fighting each other. There were two major factions of the Republican Party in New York State, and the Federalists used their internecine squabbles to their advantage during election campaigns.

At this distance, it is difficult for us to appreciate the level of animosity between the Federalists and the Democratic-Republicans in New York State at the time of the War of 1812, when desperate men took desperate measures. Even before the war, there were shady deals on both sides in an attempt to buy votes. Since only naturalized white male property owners could vote, both sides found ways to "create" more naturalized white male property owners. Fraudulent naturalizations, especially in the New York City area, lax enforcement of property requirements and spurious quitclaim deeds produced more and more voters for each side. St. Lawrence County was not immune to this phenomenon and adopted an "if you can't beat 'em, join 'em" attitude. For example, in the gubernatorial election of

Nathan Ford.

1814, 868 men out of a total of 789 qualified voters cast their ballots for a final voter turnout of 110 percent.[3] You can't be any more civic minded than that.

Nathan Ford was uniquely suited to the role of conqueror and civilizer. He was proud, ambitious, vain, utterly profane in his language[4] and undoubtedly had the personal courage required to forge a civilization out of the wilderness. Although other parts of St. Lawrence County were being developed and settled, Ford was there first, and when Ogdensburgh was designated the seat for the new county in 1802, he made sure that he and Ogdensburgh were the center of attention.

Under the New York State constitution of the time, judges (and, for that matter, most county-level officials) were appointed by the four-man Council of Appointments in Albany. This is precisely the type of system a Federalist would hold dear to his heart. The Council of Appointments was made up of rich men elected by other rich men and could be relied on to make intelligent choices (meaning to choose other wealthy powerful men), whereas the uneducated mob of common voters could not. Because of this system, in 1812, Nathan Ford was serving as chief judge for St. Lawrence County, supervisor of the Town of Oswegatchie and the de facto "mayor" of Ogdensburgh (although the village did not actually incorporate until April 1817). So there he was, top dog, as it were, in all three levels of local government: county, town and village. He considered himself a cut above the common laborers and farmers who were starting to move into the county. He also considered much of the area around Ogdensburg to be his personal fiefdom and source of income.

As war loomed on the horizon, Ford and his Federalist allies railed against the stupidity of engaging the British, whether they were tied down against the French in war or not. But war came anyway in June 1812, and St. Lawrence County found itself on the front lines.

Ford always opposed the war, and he made no bones about his willingness to get along with the British. Even after the capture of Ogdensburg in February 1813, he resolved to cozy up to the British and felt it was far better to have the British officers strolling down Ford Street than to have American army officers do the same thing. Ford admitted to his brother two weeks after the capture of the village, "I do not feel apprehensive. I feel safer than when [the American commander[5]] was here. I hope they will not send any troops here. I would rather live as we do than have the force and commandant we had." He then adds that Colonel Thomas Benedict, a local militia leader, was at Sackets Harbor and that "Benedict is military mad."[6]

General Zebulon Pike.

Letters from the time make numerous references to the fact that the two "belligerents" were often entertaining each other at dinner even after the British had captured Ogdensburg. As Ogdensburg resident John Ross put it, "We are not only perfectly quiet but on a most pleasant footing. Last Friday, Judge [Ford], Capt. Arnold and self dined with our Conqueror, and yesterday some from the other side dined with Judge. I was one of the party."[7]

Word of the extent of this fraternization reached General Zebulon Pike at Sackets Harbor by the end of March 1813, and he and Ford were already embroiled in a controversy of their own, so there was no love lost between them. Pike had sent warning to the British commander at Kingston that he should prohibit the officers at Prescott from coming over to Ogdensburg under the protection of a flag of truce and that henceforward, any British officer coming to Ogdensburg would be captured and detained as a prisoner of war. This, of course, did not sit well with His Lordship Ford, who wrote to his brother complaining of the fact on April 2, 1813. He also told John Ross that the American leadership was a pack of scoundrels and that he would write to Pike explaining to him "how beneficial intercourse is to us and of what importance to all poor sufferers here as the British will probably pay our claims [brought against the British for their sack of the village a month earlier] and would certainly have done so, at least in great part, if we had not so shamefully overstated the value of our losses."[8] Pike or no Pike, Nathan Ford was not to be confined. John Ross mentions that just a few days after the sacking of Ogdensburg, Ford requested Ross to accompany him on a visit to see Colonel MacDonell at Prescott.[9]

In a letter appearing in the *Utica Patriot* on April 27, 1813 (but probably reprinted from the *Ogdensburgh Palladium*), a thinly disguised Nathan Ford, above the signature "A St. Lawrence Farmer," wrote:

> *Our enemies since the 22nd of Feb. have certainly extended to us generosity, and we should be wanting in candor if we deny it, because we have not been marauded upon or insulted. It is a notorious fact that we have been and still are indebted to their clemency for the peace and quiet we at this moment enjoy. We have seen no disposition on the part of our government to protect us or to meliorate our condition. We are considered as a people left to ourselves and as no longer worthy of the patronage and protection of the government.*

Ford found it convenient to leave out the fact that that was exactly the way he wanted it.

This coziness may have gone a long way toward engendering the charges of treason later faced by Ford. But he was certainly not the only one willing to cede the St. Lawrence to the British as a payment for peace, nor was he the only one willing to trade with the enemy. British adjutant Noah Freer, stationed at Kingston, mentions very matter-of-factly that the Americans were willing to supply the British with provisions: "It is, however, rumoured that wheat is available in Ogdensburg for $12 per barrel. We shall be under the necessity of getting most of our flour and pork from their side."[10]

Ford was not in Ogdensburg on the day of its capture, and his home, as well as David Parish's, was left unharmed even though it was vacant. As the two grandest homes in the village, they would have been a looter's dream come true. This fact caused Ford to do some public-relations damage control. In a report that was carried in all the major newspapers of the day, General Dearborn mentioned the fact that Ford's home was spared and hinted that a British sentry had been posted there to prevent looting. Ford went on the offensive in the Federalist papers, listing the damage done to his other property such as the new barracks, his pleasure boat and the distillery. Still, the perception was that if he were not actually pro-British, he must certainly have been at least neutral, which is a dangerous attitude to adopt while your countrymen are dying and being captured. His public willingness to just try to get along with the British enemy did not go unnoticed. Whether justified or not, rumors were spread that Ford was passing information to the British during their frequent visits to Ogdensburg after the battle. He and John Ross, Parish's nephew, also visited the "enemy" and reportedly had enjoyable evenings with the British command.[11] Because of these rumors, General Dearborn, in command at Sackets Harbor, decided to take action to stop the "improper communications"[12] with the British. Although he could apparently not stop the fraternization between Prescott and Ogdensburg (he had no troops of any kind stationed in St. Lawrence County after the capture of Ogdensburg) in March 1813, he asked for and received help in the form of an "agent": Dr. Samuel Shaw of Castleton, Vermont, who was recommended by Secretary of War John Armstrong as a man who could at least stop treasonous communication by mail.

In the summer of 1813, Nathan Ford was getting more and more frustrated with the war and his lack of ability to keep the local Federalists in line with his orthodoxy. The *Ogdensburgh Palladium* editor, John Sheldon, apparently abandoned his post and told his son to stop any subscriptions with "foreign" addresses. Ford did not know this, even though he had been the de-facto editor for two months. He finally ceased publication, at least temporarily, claiming that he was not getting the support that he deserved from the "milk and water Federalists" who did not have the "spunk" to carry it on. He also believed that David Parish was getting nervous about all the criticism of the army and administration that showed up weekly in the *Palladium* and that Parish (who owned the press) would cease publication for good rather than risk army intervention, which in Ford's words would "lead to a rumpus."[13] He even accused Alexander Richards, the Democratic customs collector, of travelling to Sackets Harbor with copies of the *Palladium* to prove the disloyalty of Ogdensburg in general and Ford specifically.

One interesting example of Ford's intercourse with the enemy was his warning British colonel Pearson in Prescott of a counterfeiter who Ford believed lived north of Brockville some distance. Ford warned him that the forger was really very good and that trapping him should be considered a priority. He ended his note by requesting that Pearson immediately destroy the operation, which to history's great advantage, he did not.[14] Ford, of course, was not alone in his intercourse with the British. William Gilkison of Prescott was busily engaged in trying to buy flour and pork from merchants in Ogdensburg, claiming that the roads were in such bad shape on his side of the river that he could not get any from his own area.[15]

In the fall of 1813, as General James Wilkinson amassed his army and flotilla at Sackets Harbor, rumors were rife as to his ultimate objective. In his letters to his brother David at this time, Ford mentions information he has gleaned from "flags" sent over from the British at Prescott. He knew which British regiments were heading upriver and reported them to his brother using their regimental designation. The average person watching troop movements with a telescope would not have had that sort of information, and its source could have been only British officers who felt they could trust Ford with sensitive information. Whether or not Ford reciprocated is a matter of pure conjecture.

Nathan Ford was nobody's fool, and even though it was well known that he consorted with the British, it made no sense to be overly public about it. As John Ross wrote concerning going over to Canada with Ford, "The Court then sits and makes it prudent for the Judge and myself to be cautious."[16]

In letter after letter, Ford has nothing but criticism and disdain for the American military leadership and the party of the president. Yet he is capable of compliments, and he constantly showers them on the British at Prescott who have allowed the residents of Ogdensburg to live in peace: "Col. Morrison is much of a gentleman who commands at Prescott. He has done everything to promote our safety."[17]

In any event, Nathan Ford, without any military training as far as is known, had some choice words about General Wilkinson, the administration and their grand strategy—or lack thereof. His letters make entertaining reading even two centuries after they were postmarked. His spelling was erratic, but there was nothing erratic about his intellect. In September 1813, he wrote, "Poor little half-starved Upper Canada holds in check the whole phalanx of Democracy," and later to his brother on November 5, "If there is any system in the present movements, it must pass for a new idea in tactics. It is one that no man of ordinary capacity could easily conceive. Those who have planned and thus far carried it into operation ought to have a patent right for superior stupidity."[18] Another gem concerns the practice of drafted men hiring substitutes: "The volunteers bid up from $50 to $100 for any substitute who will take their patriotism off their hands."[19]

When "Capering Wilkinson" (as Ford called him) finally did set his invasion plan in motion, it was already the first week of November 1813. In order to avoid the guns at Prescott, he had the army offloaded above Ogdensburg and then had them march around the village to reembark on the boats downstream from the big guns at Prescott.

Responding to what he considered to be personal attacks upon his character, Ford publicly returned the favor with a scathing letter to Wilkinson that was widely reprinted in the Federalist press. The attack in the press did not go unnoticed by Wilkinson, who was licking his wounds in Malone, New York, after his resounding defeat at Crysler's Farm. He seems to have caused a subordinate to respond to Ford's attack with a reciprocal attack on Ford, which was printed in the *National Intelligencer* on December 30, 1813, under a dateline of "Malone, Dec. 7, 1813." Predictably, the Democratic press was less than sympathetic to these personal attacks. As a Balston Spa paper put it, "Judge Ford of St. Lawrence County is well known in our present age, as was Benedict Arnold in the Revolutionary War."[20] In another letter to his brother on December 17, 1813, Ford mocks Wilkinson's "accomplishments" by stating that the army "still retain possession of the salmon fishery at the old French Mills—I hope we shall have salmon cheap and plenty in the spring."[21]

The situation got even more interesting. A tavern keeper named Arnold Smith in Morristown swore out a deposition in Malone on December 6,

1813, accusing Nathan Ford and John Ross of collusion with the enemy. In the deposition, Smith stated that after Wilkinson's army passed by Ogdensburg the month before, some military stores were left in Ogdensburg and were hidden so that the British could not find them. Specifically, two mortars were hidden in a ditch and covered with hay, while several casks of clothing and blankets were secreted in the Lewis and Swanstead store. He accused John Ross of leading a British officer to Ford's mansion by a circuitous route, pointing out to him the hidden stores as they walked.[22] The British left and returned an hour later with a gunboat and demanded the public property. The mortars and casks proved too much for the gunboat in a single load, so the British took two Ogdensburg residents as hostages and came back for a second load. Smith also claimed that he had gone over to Canada in May 1813 to obtain intelligence and that Nathan Ford gave his name to a man named Jones, a Canadian partisan who reported Smith to the British authorities.[23]

Ford's older brother David responded in kind with his own defense of the judge in a long public letter, and it appears that the two men sued each other for defamation, with the case dragging on for some time.[24] David Ford claimed that Arnold Smith had a grudge against Judge Ford—that he had been caught with goods he had plundered from the Canadians and that Nathan Ford had condemned him publicly for his actions. Smith's charges were merely a transparent attempt to get back at Nathan, according to David Ford.

Another affidavit surfaced a month later when a certain John Pettis, who claimed to be a natural-born U.S. citizen forced into British service at Prescott, swore that it was common knowledge that Nathan Ford furnished the British commandant with information about the American army. He had heard Lieutenant Colonel John Colburne say that if it were not for Judge Ford, there would not be a house standing in Ogdensburg; that his services were so essential to His Majesty that they did not wish to injure his property. He said that he was in the party commanded by Captain Lauden on November 8, 1813, when they took considerable U.S. property from Ogdensburg—including two mortars, twenty-three barrels of pork and whiskey, blankets, etc.—and that Judge Ford showed them where those stores were hidden.[25]

On the last day of 1813, *The Columbian* of New York City ran an item that reported in part: "Depositions have been made and published which impeach the judge with holding treasonable correspondence with our enemies, furnishing them with information and provisions, betraying public property into their hands, and other acts of hostility against his own country.

He will have to appear in his own defence at the tribunal of justice against the charge of treason."[26] Nathan Ford was about to pay the price for following his own personal foreign policy.

Soon, other charges against Ford, which were never attributed to anyone, were appearing in the Republican press. The oft-heard accusation of passing sensitive information was joined by a new one claiming that Ford had signaled the British during Wilkinson's descent of the St. Lawrence in November 1813 by hanging blue lights in the top-most windows of his mansion. The president's party in Congress took these charges very seriously and even pondered changing the legal definition of treason so that it might have a pretext to arrest Ford and others. In Congress in January 1814, Representative Wright of New Jersey protested against this attempt to target specific people for alleged specific crimes. In part, he said:

> *Among these imaginary traitors, a most respectable inhabitant of the state in which I reside has been named. In a manner noble, generous and conclusive and worthy of his exalted character, my honorable friend from New Jersey has repelled the insinuation. Sir, the honorable gentleman arraigned, Judge Ford, is the presiding judge of the county to which he belongs. His character is exalted above all suspicion. Is there any ground for suspicion against him? Why has he not been arrested? There, in proud defiance he stands ready to answer any charge of his country.*[27]

He did not have to wait long. In mid-January 1814, Henry Brockholst Livingston, Federal Circuit Court judge in New York, issued a warrant for Nathan Ford's arrest on a charge of treason. Ford was arrested on Monday, January 24, 1814, at sword point either by two army officers or a federal marshal and brought four hundred miles to New York City in a sleigh.[28] He was arraigned on charges of high treason on January 31, 1814, in front of Judge Livingston and freed on bail, having enlisted the legal help of the firm Harrison, Wells, Emmett and Hoffman.[29]

Opinions of Ford and quickness to condemn him split predictably along party lines. The *Cooperstown Federalist* wrote:

> *This gentleman has made himself very obnoxious to the "powers that be" by an honest declaration of his political principles and a decided hostility to their views in the prosecution of an unnecessary, impolitic and ruinous war. His life has frequently been threatened by the military, but never until within a few days has he been seized and manacled by the strong arm*

> *of power. We are informed that he was lately arrested by order of the government and yesterday arrived in Utica, where he is guarded by "gens de armes."*[30]

The *New Hampshire Sentinel* added, "This step is probably to gratify the malice of Gen. Wilkinson, who could not feel very easy under the caustic lash applied by the Judge not long since."[31]

A letter written on January 30, 1814, sums up the feelings of most of the people around Oswegatchie:

> *You cannot be ignorant of the Judge's arrest. Astonishment at the past and apprehension for the future is depicted on the countenance of every honest man. With regard to the personal outrage committed upon the Judge, but one sentiment pervades all ranks, all classes, that it was arbitrary and unjust. The peace and tranquility of this county have the most serious consequences to apprehend from his absence at this critical time. Villainy, I fear, will shortly reign triumphant. But I will not anticipate greater misfortune than what we are already doomed to suffer. May it speedily be in his power to confront his persecutors, and there is no fear as to the result.*[32]

While in New York City, and later in Albany, Ford made the rounds of his political friends and tried to gauge their support. His Federalist allies were to a man convinced that the charges were trumped up and the result of Jacobin machinations. He also spread his story concerning Wilkinson's behavior the previous November and his reaction to being sued by him. He wrote from Schenectady, "This evening I spent at Judge Kent's, where I fell in with Gen. Lewis. I had considerable conversation upon the subject of the blue lights and Wilkinson. He [General Lewis] ridicules the idea of the blue lights but tried to vindicate the character of Wilkinson. But he had to acknowledge that he was a little slewed on the night he passed Ogdensburg."[33]

Ford returned north and was surprised by the level of support he found among the residents of the county. After all the expense and public embarrassment that he had gone through, the charges were dropped for lack of evidence on April 5, 1814.

By the fall of 1814, Ford—and the country—was weary of a war without tangible gains in more than two years of fighting. The New England states were considering breaking away from the United States and forming their own confederation. Ford sympathized with their feelings, writing, "I consider myself that the political dissolution of this country is close at hand."[34] When negotiations with the British were broken off, it propelled Ford into a deep funk. Like others, he was tired of the endless, aimless war, and without American protection, he felt certain the British would overrun St. Lawrence County. Fort Sullivan, near Eastport, Maine, had recently been similarly overrun, and the inhabitants were forced to take an oath of allegiance to the British Crown. Although thoroughly opposed to the war, Ford was, after all, a veteran himself, and the thought of total personal capitulation to the British monarch was too much to bear:

> *I look for a vindictive war. Should they press our frontier further interior, what are we to do? Will they not demand of the inhabitants the same as at Eastport? If they should, this county will depopulate. My anxiety upon this subject is much awakened. How to act? I am at a loss. To take the oath is out of the question, and I presume they would not let me remain without. I shall be glad to hear from you upon this subject. If it is possible for me to remain without taking the oath, I shall consider it my duty to do it. I may save my property and much for other people.*[35]

Ford need not have worried. Even with the collapse of Napoleon and the apparent weakness of the American military position, the British accepted the terms negotiated at Ghent, Belgium, and the war came to an official close in February 1815.

Chapter 2

DAVID PARISH AND HIS MONEY TREE

David Parish has been mentioned in many books and articles in the last two hundred years, with most authors describing him as a millionaire from Germany who moved to the United States in the early 1800s. On its surface, that statement is true, but it is also somewhat misleading in that most people assume he would have had a difficult time in the United States because of the language barrier. Nothing could be further from the truth, as Parish undoubtedly thought in English and spoke it perfectly but was also fluent in German and French. His father, John Parish (1742–1829), was an enterprising Scotsman who moved to the German port city of Hamburg in the 1770s and became a naturalized citizen. He served in that city as the U.S. consul general from 1790 to 1796, the only non-American to ever have been a U.S. consul, and moved back to Bath, England, by 1808. His third son, David Parish, was born there in Hamburg in 1778 and grew up in that English-speaking household but could definitely hold his own bantering with his German playmates and with his French tutor. John Parish's daughter Henrietta married Hercules Ross, who had been a close friend of Admiral Nelson in the West Indies, and in 1785, the couple moved to Scotland, where they built the large castle named "Rossie." Parish's Ross nephews were very close to him, especially after the death of their mother in 1811, and there is a wealth of surviving correspondence between the nephews and their favorite uncle.

Parish's international business started in 1806 when he established a commercial house in Antwerp, Belgium, under the auspices of Prince

David Parish. *Courtesy of St. Lawrence University Special Collections.*

Talleyrand himself. He made his real fortune assisting the Barings of London in the transfer of Spanish gold from Vera Cruz, Mexico, to New Orleans and then to French coffers, all against the British embargo but with their tacit approval. This was the result of Spain needing to pay Napoleon a huge sum, and the vast fortune of Spanish gold was still held in Mexico. In order to be closer to the action on the bullion deal, Parish moved to the United States in January 1806, first settling in New York and later moving to 153 Walnut Street in Philadelphia. His "cut" of the bullion operation was a cool $1 million dollars, which was serious money at the time.

Gouverneur Morris, a family friend who had spent quite a bit of time with David's father in the mid-1790s, introduced him to the idea of speculating in the wild, unsettled lands of northern New York. On December 2, 1808, Parish used $363,000.00 of his profits from the bullion trade to buy 200,000 acres of land from Morris, James D. LeRay and New York City lawyer David B. Ogden. His purchase included the present-day towns of Parishville, Hopkinton and Rossie in St. Lawrence County, plus part of Antwerp in Jefferson County. Buying at about $1.80 per acre, he hoped to sell to settlers for $5.00 to $6.00 per acre, depending on location and nearness to roads. After the land purchase of 1808, Parish returned to Europe to look after business but returned the next year to develop his holdings in the North Country. He differed from almost all the great land barons of the time in that he actually had an interest in developing and settling the lands rather than just making a profit through land speculation. Over the next few years, Parish invested huge amounts of money to make his holdings accessible by road and to develop the newly discovered iron ore deposits in Rossie.

Although Parish had grand plans for his property in St. Lawrence County, the truth was that he had grand plans for everything he owned and had many other business ventures that included international commerce and money lending. He realized very quickly that he would need a resident business manager to oversee his interests in the North Country during the majority of the year when he was either at home in Philadelphia or traveling in the United States or Europe. Joseph Rosseel of Ghent, Belgium, was recommended to him, and the two men formed a partnership that resulted in Rosseel working for the Parish family for more than a half century.

At this early time, Parish contracted with Joseph Jacques Ramee to design a manor house for him in Ogdensburg. Joseph Rosseel arranged with master builder Daniel W. Church to begin the project in the spring of 1809. It took up a majority of the block between Ford, Caroline, Euphemia (now called State Street) and Washington Streets in Ogdensburg and was constructed of nearly 400,000 locally made bricks of "blue" clay. On April 8, 1809, Parish met with David B. Ogden in New York City and bought from him all the unsold lots in the village of Ogdensburg for $8,000.[36]

Shipwrights were already in place in January 1809, having built a shed under which to complete two schooners for Parish and Co. At the same time, red cedar logs for the ships' keel and knees were being cut down and sawn. Captain Obed Mayo, Parish's nautical advisor, arrived in Ogdensburg in early June 1809 with all the rigging necessary for the schooners. He had purchased it in New York and on its way north "took as much care of it as Roman Catholicks do their relicks."[37] The first completed schooner, the *Experiment*, was launched on the Fourth of July 1809, being a centerpiece of the local Independence Day celebrations attended by about four hundred people. It was of fifty tons burthen and required six and a half feet of draft, with a sixty-four-foot main mast and a sixty-one-foot foremast.[38] At a picnic dinner that afternoon attended by ninety-six people, Judge Nathan Ford felt compelled to offer the following toast to the man who made it all happen:

"To David Parish Esquire—may his commercial enterprises be as successful on the St. Lawrence as they were on the ocean."[39] Later in the summer, a second, slightly smaller schooner, the *Collector*, began its career on the river[40] and was ultimately owned by Joseph Rosseel. Soon, Captain Obed Mayo had also completed his boat, the *Genesee Packet*.[41]

Having David Parish Esq. even as a part-time resident was very beneficial to the year-rounders in Ogdensburg. Case in point: Parish was able to use his influence in Washington to have the mail delivered from DeKalb every week instead of fortnightly. This arrangement was a huge advantage to the local business interests, which of course included Parish and Co. itself.[42]

Parish was not unaware that the St. Lawrence River traffic was split into two completely different regimes. The deep-water boats such as the ones he had built and which delivered goods to his store from all the ports on Lake Ontario were only half of the shipping business—the half that Ogdensburg and Prescott were later to specialize in. The other half was the downriver trade of raw materials to Montreal, which was just as lucrative but involved building sturdy rafts that could be connected together on their way downstream. These "arks," as they were called, would be large enough to have a little cook shanty on one, as the trip took several days. Their advantage was that they were of very shallow draft and could be broken up into their smaller components so that they could run the various rapids more nimbly than a large raft. David Parish was very competitive, but he knew he could not do well in the downriver traffic unless he could learn the secrets of raft building the way the merchants in Kingston built them. So until he had mastered the art of raft making, Parish and Co. would have to satisfy themselves with the deep-water shipping business.[43]

Joseph Rosseel looked over the town of Rossie for Parish in 1812 and confirmed earlier reports of iron deposits near Somerville. The initial discovery was made by surveyors who noticed the erratic behavior of their compass needles. A crew of men was sent there to excavate a sample of ore, which was sent to Fairfield Academy in Herkimer County for assaying. The results came back quite promising, so Parish ordered two men—Gophar Holden and William Harris, of Antwerp—to make a four-rod-wide road from Somerville to the site of Rossie village, at the head of Black Lake, so that a blast furnace could be located there. He also ensured that the Ogdensburg Turnpike would connect his furnace with the port at Ogdensburg.

Once news of the war reached Ogdensburg in June 1812, Parish immediately wrote to Paul Hamilton, the secretary of the U.S. Navy,

Joseph Rosseel. *Courtesy of the Ogdensburg Public Library.*

and offered him the lease of his three fast schooners, which were then in Ogdensburg harbor.[44] One of these schooners, the *Experiment*, was leased to the U.S. government in 1812, converted to a five-gun boat plying the waters of Lake Ontario under the command of Mervin P. Mix and rechristened the *Growler* (not to be confused with the larger ship by the same name on Lake Champlain).[45]

On October 4, 1812, the British and Canadians made a half-hearted attempt to cross the St. Lawrence and take Ogdensburg. By the time they got midway across the river, they tired of American grapeshot and abandoned the effort. David Parish, who watched the travesty from his waterfront store, quickly wrote to Governor Tompkins and asked that he send more troops for the protection of Ogdensburg. Tompkins replied that he understood his concern but that it would be at least until spring before he could send any reinforcements. Parish was quite sure that the Americans would ultimately triumph though, because Britain was far too occupied with Napoleon to send enough military resources to finish the job in North America. He wrote to his father in England that sooner or later, the Canadas would be in American hands, and then his house in Ogdensburg would "no longer stand on the frontier."

Parish left Ogdensburg not long after New Year's Day 1813 and returned to Philadelphia. In April of that year, he, along with John Jacob Astor and Stephen Girard, loaned the U.S. government $16 million for the continuation of the war. Parish wanted the war concluded as soon as possible so that the development of his lands could continue, but he simply could not resist a moneymaking opportunity like the government loan, which was made at 7.5 percent interest. He was justly accused of playing both ends against the middle. The unsettled conditions of the "front lines" essentially froze further immigration and acted as an impediment for any sort of economic development in the area. This loan did not mean the end of taxation on the states, and in August 1813, St. Lawrence County was charged $3,000 as its share of the war cost.[46]

Parish's Federalist friends all over the country were understandably aghast at this loan. A bankrupt American government would have had no choice but to conclude some sort of peace treaty. But Parish could not resist the financial rewards and the increase in his influence with the Madison administration that the loan would ensure. He was able to convince the military leaders to take their dirty little war elsewhere and leave the St. Lawrence River valley in peace. He was perhaps the main reason that the St. Lawrence never saw another federal soldier stationed there after February 1813.

William Benbow was hired to construct and oversee the workings of the iron furnace at Rossie. A clever dump ramp was constructed so that wagons would be able to dump their ore directly into the top of the furnace. The initial blast was conducted on January 18, 1814, in front of Nathan Ford, Joseph Rosseel and Silvius Hoard.[47] The smelting itself was a success, but the hearth could not withstand the temperature produced and so collapsed. The ironworks was never a profit-making enterprise while Parish owned it.

However, the possibility of producing cannon shot for the American army was considered as one of the possible uses of the iron produced at Rossie, and Parish sent out feelers to the War Department to ascertain their interest. He met with Colonel Decius Wadsworth, commissary general for ordnance, on February 16, 1813, and wrote Joseph Rosseel that he very likely would make a contract with him for the production of cannonballs for the U.S. Army.[48] He later gave Wadsworth a price of $80 per ton, or $85 per ton if delivered to Ogdensburg, and informed Commodore Isaac Chauncey at Sackets of the same price.[49] By May of that year, he had written to Joseph Rosseel telling him that he had delayed getting into a contract with the army until "the frontier is secure from the incursions of the British."[50]

Parish's iron furnace is the long white building just above the tree in the foreground.

When reading the above account of Parish's interest in St. Lawrence County, one would assume that he had developed a special fondness or loyalty to his adopted county. But by the beginning of the second year of the war, his true loyalties became apparent. In mid-June 1813, Parish made a trip from Ogdensburgh to his home in Philadelphia and from there went on to Washington, D.C., to hobnob with those in power and to further his own interests. He was warmly welcomed there, with those in government keenly aware of their reliance on his loan two months previously. While in Washington, he would probably have been entertained by the secretaries of war and treasury at the very least, as well as other high-ranking men in the administration. He headed back north in early August and arrived in Ogdensburg by the eighth of that month.[51]

In the incident that followed, it is interesting to note that the British across the river knew where Parish had been and when he had returned to Ogdensburg. Whether a non-citizen can be called a traitor or not is a matter of semantics, but British colonel Thomas Pearson's letter of August 9, 1813, leaves little doubt that when David Parish was faced with the choice of backing the British or backing the Americans, he came down squarely on the side of backing David Parish. Following is the text of Pearson's letter to the lieutenant governor of Upper Canada, Sir George Prevost, dated August 9, 1813, written within a day or two of

Parish's return. It references an incident during the Napoleonic Wars in which Parish played a leading role, but more interestingly, it also proves the depths of Parish's treachery in dealing with the enemy and hints that the British spy William Gilkison of Prescott had acted in his capacity of spy handler more than once.[52] Note Pearson's use of an elementary cipher to "disguise" Parish's name, even though he named Parish in the very first line of the letter:

> *Sir,*
>
> *Mr. Parish's arrival from Washington induced me to send over Mr. Gilkison to Ogdensburg with a view of procuring such political information as Mr. P. might think proper to communicate, and knowing the former intimacy which existed between these two gentleman, I was in hopes of gleaning something which might probably be not uninteresting to Your Excellency.*
>
> *Such is the substance which I have collected from Mr. Gilkison, and it is not improbable that by his means I may be enabled to learn something still more interesting, as Mr. WHYPZO has had access and confidential interviews with those at the head of the United States Government.*
>
> *With respect to our force, he adds that there has not been more than 3,000 men at Sackets Harbour, and these are very sickly, and further says that from information direct from General Lewis, it is understood that their armies are incapable of any further offensive operations. The army at Fort George is very sickly, their effective strength were 3,000 and in great dread of a general attack. The war daily becomes more unpopular, and the* [illegible] *does not keep pace with their hopes.*[53]

Apologists may say that Parish did not betray any American war plans as such, so there is no cause to accuse him of treachery. But in the intelligence world, even the knowledge of an enemy's *inaction* is a valuable advantage—one that would allow the British to move troops away from certain defensive positions and to pursue their own offensive plans. And the cause of Parish's perfidy? Profit. The very next day after Pearson's coded letter, Parish wrote to him. He wanted to ensure that the British would leave his iron furnace in Rossie alone, writing that his furnace was a civilian-use-only enterprise and that the iron produced would be used for "country purposes" only.[54] He appealed directly to the governor of Upper Canada to make sure his property was not harmed:

Ogdensburgh
County of St. Lawrence
Aug. 10, 1813

Dear Sir,

It is, I believe, already known to you that I am erecting ironworks on my lands at the head of Black Lake about 25 miles from this place on which subject I beg leave respectfully to submit to you the following observations and to request the favor of you to communicate them to His Excellency Sir George Prevost.

Having discovered very valuable iron ore on my lands last year, I made immediate arrangements for the erection of a furnace and other necessary appendages, which works were commenced during the last summer soon after the declaration of war with a view of benefitting my lands and doing country work only.

As it is not unlikely that mis-representations may have gone abroad and that the erection of works of this description so near the lines may be viewed with a suspicious eye by his Britanick Majesty's Commission in Canada, I am very desirous of making Sir George Prevost acquainted with the true state of the case and of conveying through you to His Excellency an assurance that no contract has been made or shall be entered into by me with the Government of the United States or any of its agents for the manufacture and delivery of implements of war by the said works during the continuation of the existing hostilities between this country and Great Britain and that my word of honour is to be considered as herewith most solemnly pledged for the faithful performance of said engagement.

As I have not the honour of being known to His Excellency, I shall write and request my friend Mr. Isaac Todd of Montreal to address a line to Sir George Prevost which will, I trust, be calculated to create sufficient confidence as to induce His Excellency to convey to me, through you, the assurance that the works will be considered as private property and that no molestation will be experienced in completing them.

I will consider myself under particular obligations for your kind attention to my request at your earliest convenience, as I am very desirous of receiving His Excellency's determination on the above application so that I may put a stop to the works in case the answer should not be favorable.

I cannot conclude this letter without expressing to you the grateful sense I entertain in common with all my friends here for the honourable sentiments expressed and the magnanimous conduct pursued by you as relates to the unprotected private property on this side of the St. Lawrence and that I am with great truth and regard.

Sir
Your very obedient and humble servant
David Parish

So, Parish sold out his American associates for nothing more than a smelter for horseshoes and hinges. The next in this series of nefarious notes is one from Colonel Pearson to Parish on August 14, 1813, written by a third person or handed to Parish by a messenger of some type:

Prescott
14 August 1813

Col. Pearson returns his best compliments to Mr. Parish and feels much obliged to him for his interesting papers. Col. P. has transmitted Mr. Parish's letters to Sir George Prevost, and Mr. Todd and is in hourly expectation of receiving His Excellency's reply, which shall instantly be transmitted to Ogdensburgh. Col. P most ardently hopes for a confirmation of Mr. Parish's pacific wishes.

He refers to Parish's abject begging to have his precious Rossie ironworks left alone and expects that Prevost will agree. The most interesting part of the note is the ambiguous "interesting papers" that Parish gave him. We have no way of knowing whether he was simply referring to recent Philadelphia newspapers or official papers of some kind—something more sinister concerning the American army.

At last, on August 16, 1813, Parish's perfidy paid off:

Prescott
16 August 1813

Sir,

I have the honor to send you the following extract of a letter received yesterday from the Secretary of His Excellency the Commander of the Forces dated Kingston 14th August 1813.

> *"I am directed by His Excellency the Commander of the Forces* [Sir George Prevost] *to acquaint you that in reply to Mr. Parish's letter of the 10th inst. which you have transmitted to him, you may give him the assurance that, relying upon the honorable pledge he has given with regard to the ironworks he is erecting, His Excellency is willing to consider them as private property and to extend the same protection to them which the private property of the subjects of the United States have invariably experienced from him during the course of the present war."*[55]

David Parish's loyalty was solidly on the side of making money. His nephew, John Ross, had obviously been communicating with the British on behalf of his uncle and received a letter from Colonel George MacDonell in Kingston the following month. MacDonell referred to speaking with Sir George Prevost about respecting Parish's property (meaning the ironworks at Rossie) and said that it would not be molested "if not forced by wanton aggression to retaliate...and the Adjutant General assured me a fortnight since that it has been intimated to Col. Pearson that Mr. Parish's property should suffer no injury under those conditions."[56] Note that MacDonell was the British commander who had sacked Ogdensburg earlier that year.

The fact that munitions were at least considered even after the exchange of letters above is borne out by a note to Parish from John Ross on March 26, 1814, in which he mentions that he had received the molds for cannon shot from the Ogdens and had used them to try out Parish's outdoor bowling alley (*kegelbahn*) and that they and the bowling grounds performed admirably.

Parish did seem to be able to have it both ways. His money financed the war and made him a handsome profit, and he made sure through his influence that the war he financed would take place somewhere far away from his little piece of America. Financing the destruction of other peoples' property did not bother him in the least.

In 1814, word got around about the continued possibility of Parish's ironworks producing munitions, and the British sent a party of soldiers to Rossie, ostensibly to chase down horse thieves but in reality to evaluate the rumors of a munitions-producing iron smelter right under their noses. They stayed at Horatio Berthrong's tavern in Rossie. A second similar mission took place in the summer of 1814 under the leadership of Captain Thomas Fraser. The threat that his smelter might be destroyed convinced Parish that any profit from cannonballs would not be worth risking the entire venture.

Treason can take many forms, and "aiding and abetting the enemy" may not strictly have to do with military secrets or outright assistance in battle. Case in point: the Americans attacked and burned York (Toronto) in April 1813 and did not just satisfy themselves with capturing military stores, continuing on a rampage of arson and destruction that served no military purpose whatsoever (and in doing so provided the British with the excuse to burn Washington, D.C., in 1814). They burned public buildings, including the Upper Canada Parliament buildings, and destroyed the government's printing press.

In a letter written to Parish in German by John Ross in April 1814, a mention was made of selling the old *Ogdensburgh Palladium* printing press to the British government in Kingston,[57] which was serving as the provincial capital until Toronto could be rebuilt. This press had been used by the *Palladium* and brought to Ogdensburg through the offices of Parish and Co. in 1810. In March 1814, Sir Gordon Drummond had made official arrangements to buy this press for £84 7s 6d,[58] considering it a personal favor from Parish. John Ross mentioned getting Colonel Pearson in Prescott to come over and get it using a horse that had been stolen from the other side. This was not a printing press for use in newspaper publishing—the *Kingston Gazette* published once a week on a perfectly serviceable press. The sole purpose of the Ogdensburg press was to print British government warrants, military decrees and official notices in service of His Britannic Majesty, so it is no wonder that Ross's letter was in German. On April 6, 1814, Parish's Canadian acquaintance and part-time spy William Gilkison took possession of the press and was ready to send it, packed in five crates, to Kingston. He noted that the type for the press was packed in twenty-two small boxes but that there was no ink included for the press itself.[59]

Gil Smissaert ran Parish's operations in the town of Parishville, and much has been made of his congratulating him on the burning of Washington, D.C., in September 1814. Although Parish was certainly not what we would call a patriot, he also had no particular wish for the ruination of the country, especially since it owed him millions of dollars. Parish just wanted to make money, and the full text of what Smissaert said indicates that Parish's joy at the burning of the city simply meant that he would not have to make the tiring journey to that dull, humid, muddy, backwater of a town. Smissaert wrote: "I wish you joy with the destruction of Washington as much for the general as for your individual good and comfort. This will save you a most damnable jaunt."[60]

Parish's mansion in Ogdensburg had been made of locally fired bricks, and the British apparently felt they did not have access to the same quality clay and kilns. As a result, in late 1814, as they were expanding and

Canadian businessman and spy William Gilkison.
Courtesy of the University of Guelph.

improving the capabilities of Fort Wellington, they began to obtain bricks from Ogdensburg, with Parish's nephew John Ross arranging the transfer. Although direct business with the enemy was carried on by many, it was still considered bad form to do it in public. Therefore, John Ross arranged to have loads of four thousand bricks at a time left at Mile Point just below the village, and he would replace them whenever he noticed that a load had been picked up. This arrangement apparently worked well enough for a while, but it seems that the commandant at Prescott became impatient in December 1814 and sent over a boat with a crew of six to pick up bricks directly—a little difficult to explain in broad daylight. And not only did they appear in broad daylight, but the weather and the river scared them enough that they did not want to re-cross the river, and so they begged Ross to be able to stay in the village overnight.[61]

One final testimony to the "cooperation" between Parish and the British took place at the end of 1814. Lieutenant Humphrey Webster of the Sixth

U.S. Infantry had been very badly wounded in the head at Lundy's Lane on the Niagara peninsula and captured while unconscious and bleeding. He was brought to Kingston and then sent on his way to Quebec as a prisoner of war, waiting to be exchanged. When he got as far as Prescott, the British took pity on him and let him stay in Ogdensburg for a while. As John Ross wrote to Parish, "Col. Grant [temporary commander at Fort Wellington] said that your conduct had been so very handsome that he would at least show a wish to retaliate and sent Webster to remain in the village on parole until he can get Sir George's [Prevost] consent to do more."

In 1814, Parish and his associates Astor and Girard were hoping that the U.S. government would re-charter a second U.S. bank and that they would be the directors since they had so much personal risk tied up in the government loans. However, there was too much Congressional opposition to the new bank and it was not until 1816 that a bank was again established.

Parish left the United States in July 1816[62] to see friends and family in England and the Continent, especially his aging father. He undoubtedly planned to be gone a few months and then to return to his northern New York holdings and continue their development. However, he was convinced while in Europe to become a partner in a newly established banking house in Vienna, Frier and Co., which went bankrupt in 1825. Because he felt responsible for losing his father's fortune in the venture, he committed suicide on April 27, 1826, by drowning himself in the Danube.

Chapter 3

TWISTING THE LION'S TAIL

To a just-arrived observer, the British attack and capture of Ogdensburg in February 1813 might have seemed an inexplicable and unprovoked violent episode. In truth, the attack, although perhaps not planned very far ahead of time, was a reaction to dozens of incidents (most of them minor) that had occurred in the previous eight months since the start of the war. It is also possible to link the attack to events even further in the past—events that ended up causing the war in the first place.

The Embargo Act of December 1807 was widely disregarded by a populace that could not see any benefit at all to not trading with their neighbors and friends on the other side of the St. Lawrence. The law forbade American ships from carrying cargoes of any kind to foreign ports and was amended four months later to include overland foreign trade as well. After fourteen ineffective months, the Embargo Act was replaced by the Non-Intercourse Act, which was just as popular with the residents of St. Lawrence County and just as effective. Due to the general tendency to ignore the law, two army companies under Captains Samuel Cherry and Thomas Anderson and Lieutenant Hicks were sent to Ogdensburg to enforce the law and were in place by February 1809, charged with putting a stop to the smuggling.[63]

By all accounts, they were unwelcome guests, and the residents of St. Lawrence County were not pleased to have their profitable trade with the Canadians curtailed. It is one thing to tell someone in Maryland that they cannot trade with the British, but it is quite another thing to tell someone living on the St. Lawrence, in plain sight of their friends and relatives across the river, that they can no longer buy and sell as they had since the settlement of the river valley began. Not only were the troops officious and heavy-handed in their enforcement of the hated embargo, but they also put a strain on the community by consuming large quantities of food. What they could not buy, they stole. Joseph Rosseel complained that they were nothing but a "banditti of rapscallions, who, by nocturnal excursions in our village, carry off pigs, geese, chickens, potatoes, onions, etc."[64] These rapscallions finally left Ogdensburg on May 31, 1809, and not a tear was shed by them nor their erstwhile "hosts."

Between the Non-Intercourse Act and perhaps just a bad harvest, 1809 was not a pleasant year in the Ogdensburg area. In the spring, Rosseel wrote to Parish that the inability to trade with the Canadians was causing a food shortage and that "I believe the Administration intends starving us." Later that year, he mentioned that there was no bread to be had in the village and that they were anxiously awaiting the schooner *Experiment* from Sodus, New York, with a load of wheat. Until that time, he said they had been reduced to eating rice "like the Bengals."[65] Louis Hasbrouck distributed one hundred bushels of wheat to be repaid when the *Experiment* returned (hopefully) with provisions.

The New York State legislature passed a bill on February 24, 1809, directing the governor to select a site where an arsenal could be built, well back from the frontier, and large enough to hold five hundred stands of arms. Russell Attwater, a wealthy landowner and proprietor of the Town of Russell, let it be known that he would donate the land for a thirty-foot by fifty-foot arsenal on the edge of the village of Russell,[66] where he lived and whose development was crucial to his investment. The governor agreed, and both sides profited from the bargain. New York State got an arsenal close enough to the Canadian frontier to be useful but not so close as to be an easy target. Attwater may have gotten the better end of the bargain, since the presence of an arsenal in Russell would ultimately force the state to connect that arsenal (and, of course, its nearby village) with an all-weather road constructed at government expense. This road, originally called the St. Lawrence Turnpike but later called the Russell Turnpike, was begun as a private moneymaking venture that incorporated in April 1810 and was intended to run from the town of Wilna in Jefferson County to Malone in Franklin County. However, in 1813, it was relieved of the burden of continuing any further east than Bangor in Franklin County.

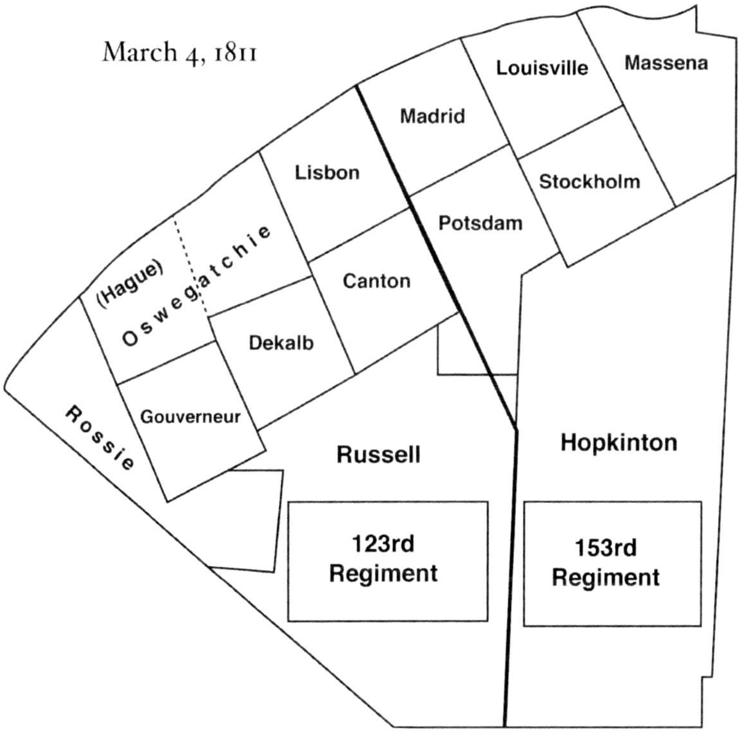

Militia designations used during the war.

On March 4, 1811, St. Lawrence County was split into two militia regiments. A line was drawn down between the townships of Madrid and Lisbon, then continuing south following the line that divided Macomb's Purchase Lots 2 and 3 to the southern border of the county. All the towns west of that line were in the 123rd New York Militia, and everything to the east was placed in the new 153rd New York Militia Regiment.

Even a quick glance at a map of the St. Lawrence River and Great Lakes would suggest to an amateur strategist that if the St. Lawrence were controlled, British forces around the lakes would be cut off from supplies sent from Montreal and England and become quite helpless. A more detailed look at the river would show that Ogdensburg would be the perfect harbor from which this total control of the river could be effected. The St. Lawrence is only a mile wide there, and Ogdensburg had a reasonably good harbor. Therefore, ships with real firepower could be used at Ogdensburg and on the lakes instead of the smaller gunboats and Durham boats needed to navigate the rapids downstream.

Although the area around modern-day Prescott, Ontario, had been settled as early as 1785, there was no real village there until about April 1811, when several houses were begun. The reason Prescott was established was that it was the last place on the St. Lawrence River where deep draft boats could navigate before encountering the first of five sets of rapids as the river falls down to Montreal. Therefore, Prescott was established as a freight-forwarding post where down-bound supplies were transferred off the larger boats to small, flat-bottomed boats, and the reverse process occurred with shipments heading upriver into the lakes. By the beginning of the war, there were only about twenty houses in the village, with far more British soldiers in the area than civilians. So, the Americans started out with numerical superiority and could have easily controlled the flow of British men and materiel if they had tried.

In hindsight, it certainly does seem odd that the U.S. government would fritter away so much time and effort on the periphery of the battlefield while leaving the heart of the matter practically undefended. Aware as it was of local opposition to the war, and therefore unable to count on large numbers of enthusiastic militia, a strong force of regular army could have been positioned along the St. Lawrence frontier to choke off British supplies to the interior of the continent and ultimately to invade Canada, if that were the original object of the war.

Tension was rising during the spring of 1812, and Governor Tompkins ordered the drafting of the state militia. The New York State militia in the area were overseen by General Jacob Brown of Jefferson County, and the ranking officer in the St. Lawrence County regiment was Lieutenant Colonel (soon to be General)[67] Thomas B. Benedict of DeKalb.[68] In preparation for possible hostilities, Brown ordered Benedict to gather forty-three men at Old DeKalb and be ready for action at a moment's notice. St. Lawrence County called up its militia on May 5, 1812, all to be in active service for six months. These men, plus other draftees amounting to a total of about eighty men, marched to Ogdensburg and took up quarters in the courthouse until more suitable housing could be built.

General Jacob Jennings Brown.

Militia from other counties, as well as St. Lawrence, were also activated and sent to Ogdensburg in case they were needed. Captain Darius Hawkins was from Herkimer County but commanded a company in Ogdensburg in 1812, and many of the men in that company were from St. Lawrence County. However, most of the militia present at Ogdensburg in the early days of the war were from other counties. The companies of Jost Bell and Jacob Weber were from Herkimer County, Nathan Cook and Jacob Hovey's were from Lewis County, Imri Case led a company from Oswego Co. and Nathan Adams from Oneida, with Giles Kellogg from Schoharie County.

Elisha Griffin and Moses Bunnell also commanded companies at Ogdensburg, and they were purely St. Lawrence County units. Odd as it may seem, there were never to be any federal troops on the border, with the exception of the seven-month stay of Captain Benjamin Forsyth's First United States Rifles, who arrived at the end of July 1812. All the other skirmishes and border duty during the conflict were performed by New York State militia.

This influx of men to Ogdensburg, perhaps five hundred or so, required housing and other infrastructure that did not yet exist. Although parts of the

The Russell Arsenal. *Courtesy of the St. Lawrence County Historical Association.*

old French/British stone fort on the point beside the Oswegatchie River still existed, they were the property of Nathan Ford, and the surviving buildings were in no shape to hold hundreds of men. In 1810, as David Parish was building his commercial empire using schooners made in Ogdensburg, a certain General Charles Burr of Troy, New York, leased some land beside the old garrison and erected a ropewalk[69], which is a long, narrow and open-sided building used to manufacture ropes and hawsers used on ships. "He is already busy in setting his kinsman a-going who is one of the first-rate ropemakers...and ordered him from New York a couple tons of hemp to begin with."[70] The ropewalk itself had later been sold to a Mr. Hill, who in turn sold his lease in 1812 to the New York State Quartermaster General Peter Porter to be fitted up for a barracks holding two hundred men.[71] At least that was a start.

On June 18, 1812, war was declared, but the news did not reach northern New York until about June 27, when a boat brought the news from Montreal. Several companies of militia were drafted for six months' service to last until December 26, 1812, and most of these men did their service at Ogdensburg and other points on the river. They were armed with the equipment that had been stored at the New York State arsenal in Russell, which was safely away from the river and possible enemy attack.

On the day the war news arrived, there were eight commercial schooners tied up at the wharves in Ogdensburg. Fitting them up as war vessels would be as easy as mounting some cannons on them, and that fact was lost on neither the British nor the Americans, both of whom desired as much firepower as possible so as to command the river and Lake Ontario. Fearing capture by the Canadians, all eight vessels made a run for Sackets Harbor on the morning of June 29, 1812. Nineteen-year-old Dunham Jones lived in Maitland, Upper Canada, about halfway between Morristown and Ogdensburg, and when he heard what was afoot, he set out with a company of men in row boats to try and capture the fleeing ships. On the surface, this sounds like a fool's mission, but sailing against the strong spring current in a confined channel, especially with no wind or an unfavorable wind, is not easy, so small, oar-powered boats could easily overtake a becalmed larger vessel. Jones and his compatriots intercepted the unarmed flotilla a short distance upstream from Brockville and succeeded in gaining control of two of the vessels, the *Sophia* and the *Island Packet*. They emptied them of their cargoes and crews and, for some reason, burned them instead of turning them over to the British navy. The other six boats fled back downriver to the relative safety of Ogdensburg's harbor.

The U.S. forces needed those boats as much as the British, and both sides determined to go to Ogdensburg and get control of them before their opponent did. On July 18, 1812,[72] the British sent the ten-gun *Duke of Gloucester* downriver from Kingston to Prescott to join the *Prince Regent*, already in the harbor. Although tied up peacefully at the wharf at Prescott for a few days, they conveyed the unspoken threat that none of the six schooners should try another escape. They also posed a threat that they could attack the ships any time they wanted and either capture or destroy them.

On July 20, Major General Stephen van Rensselaer (a Federalist, by the way) visited Ogdensburg with the intention of constructing at least the rudiments of defensive structures, and under his direction, a battery and breastworks were begun at the east end of the village down near the shore, plus a garrison and barracks built on the grounds of Nathan Ford's old fort. This rebuilt defensive position was named Fort Rensselaer in his honor.[73] He was accompanied on this visit by his entire entourage, which included his second cousin, Lieutenant Colonel Solomon van Rensselaer.

Solomon van Rensselaer, with the cooperation of Colonel Benedict, formulated a plan to cross the river with an armed force and attack the *Duke of Gloucester* as it lay in the harbor on July 22. In the afternoon before the planned expedition, he wrote his wife a goodbye letter in which he claimed

Colonel Solomon van Rensselaer.

he would either "succeed or fall,"[74] but as luck would have it, he did neither. Although the boats were ready by 1:00 a.m. and the attack was planned for 3:00 a.m., only 66 of the 120 or so men who volunteered actually appeared for duty that night, so the mission was cancelled.[75] The lack of enthusiasm on the part of the militia may have been related to their overall reluctance to leave the borders of the state for any offensive mission. On July 30, the *Duke of Gloucester* and *Prince Regent* were joined by the sixteen-gun sloop *Earl of Moira*, and the three ships, clearly visible from the dock at Ogdensburg, waited menacingly.

The Americans knew time was wasting, so on the morning of July 29, the schooner *Julia* (which had been captured from the British and was commanded by midshipman Henry Wells) left Sackets Harbor en route to Ogdensburg with supplies and intending to escort the six remaining ships back to Sackets Harbor. A Durham boat followed the *Julia*, carrying the Jefferson County militia company of Captain Noahdiah Hubbard of Champion. Word of this movement must have made it to Prescott, because on the afternoon of July 31, the *Earl of Moira* and *Duke of Gloucester* intercepted the *Julia* just offshore of Morristown, about eleven miles upstream from Ogdensburg.

Although badly outnumbered in terms of actual cannons, the *Julia*'s massive thirty-two-pound cannon and two six-pounders caused the British to be somewhat circumspect to say the very least, and they dared not come close enough to board the *Julia*. The British boats were aided in the attack by five or six guns onshore. The two sides fired many rounds at each other, but without causing serious damage on either side. After about three hours of inconclusive fighting, the British vessels backed off toward the Canadian shore. Wells, the commander of the *Julia*, was fearful of being boarded after sundown by the many small boats carrying troops that he had noticed against the shore, so under the cover of darkness but with the aid of occasional lightning flashes for guidance, the *Julia* was towed downstream to Ogdensburg by Captain Hubbard's Durham boat and the *Julia*'s own yawl. As they passed the village of Morristown, several eighteen-pound balls from Brockville overshot the *Julia* and landed without harm in the village, two of those shells being recovered.[76] To emerge without the loss of a man after three hours of heavy shelling from a far superior force said a lot about the skill and bravery of Henry Wells and his crew. During Sir George Prevost and General Henry Dearborn's armistice from August 9 to September 4, 1812, the six remaining boats were moved from Ogdensburg to the safety of Sackets Harbor.[77]

On July 30, 1812, General van Rensselaer and his detail left Ogdensburg for Sackets Harbor, escorted by uniformed militia and given an artillery salute by Captain Darius Hawkins and his men as they crossed the bridge over the Oswegatchie. When about a mile out of town on the State Road toward Heuvelton, the procession stopped, and Colonel Benedict sent them on their way with this farewell: "Sir, on behalf of the officers and troops under my command, I return you our sincere thanks for the early attention you have bestowed on our situation, and we implore the blessings of heaven attend you through your arduous undertakings."[78]

About two weeks later, on August 11, 1812, the fortifications and barracks on the grounds of the old Fort La Presentation were completed, and Lieutenant Colonel Benedict led his troops across the bridge to dedicate them. Nathan Ford, who owned the land upon which the fort stood, had no choice but to appear in public as if he supported the decision to fortify the border. He mounted the wall by the American flag[79] and addressed the men: "Patriotic Soldiers! This fort, reared by the hands of freemen, as one link in the chain of forts necessary for the defense of our frontiers, is named Fort Van Rensselaer in testimony of that respect we all bear to Major General Van Rensselaer." Perhaps naming the fort after a good Federalist like himself made the chore more palatable. After three cheers were given, Colonel Benedict stood up on the wall to add his sentiments: "Fellow Soldiers! May this standard which is now waving over our heads, the pride and emblem of our national independence and sovereignty, be defended by the arm of Americans until those luminaries which they represent shall set in the night of time." Three more rousing cheers, and the men moved into their new quarters.[80]

Although the United States was the country that declared war, the Madison administration had no idea how to proceed and really did not have a clear vision of its war aims. It made sense to fortify the border with Canada quickly and strongly, but with what troops? They were already keenly aware of the weakness they would suffer from the continued reliance on the state militia system. The regular army was pathetically undermanned, so reliance on the state militias, many of which were controlled by governors who had little or no appetite for war, was an unfortunate necessity. And knowing full well the Federalist leanings of some locales, such as northern New York, it made sense to send a strong contingent of professional soldiers who could be counted on to prosecute the war with vigor. However, instead of a strong concentrated force, the War Department sent a single company of regulars, the First United States Rifles, under the command of North Carolina native Captain Benjamin Forsyth, to "guard" the entire St. Lawrence River valley—and specifically Ogdensburg.

Forsyth and his men arrived at Sackets Harbor on July 30, 1812, after a long and tiring journey from New York, to Albany, then to Utica and down the Black River valley. Forsyth was precisely what the senior leadership of the army was not: he was bold, decisive, personally fearless and eager for a fight anytime, anywhere. He was somewhat reckless and perhaps not the best disciplinarian, but his men loved him and were fiercely loyal to him. By September 1, he had enlisted twenty-six more recruits for five-year enlistments and ended up paying their enlistment bounties out of his own pocket, echoing a constant theme heard throughout the war: that the U.S. government neglected the very basic necessities such as pay and clothing allowances. It did not take him long to prove what kind of soldier he was. Seven weeks after his arrival on the scene, on September 21, 1812, he led a force of eighty regulars and thirty-four militiamen from Cape Vincent across the St. Lawrence and attacked Ganonoque in Upper Canada. He routed the British garrison there, capturing twelve and killing ten while losing only one of his command. They captured forty-one stands of arms, twenty-five bayonets, twenty-one cartouche boxes, nine bayonet belts and scabbards, two barrels of fixed ammunition, one barrel of powder and one barrel of flints. His men fired into the home of the local commander, Colonel Joel Stone, and wounded his wife, the only occupant at the time, and then ransacked his house.[81] This served the Canadians as an excellent introduction to Benjamin Forsyth.[82]

On October 1, 1812, General Jacob Brown arrived in Ogdensburg aboard the USS *Niagara*, supplanting Benedict as the ranking officer in the theater. The next day, forty or so boats approached Prescott from Johnstown, guarded by two British warships. Later that day, the cannon situated on the bank above the river began firing at Ogdensburg in order to cover the flotilla, causing little damage but signaling that something more sinister might be afoot. General Brown decided not to fire back, as he did not have enough gunpowder to "sport with" at such long distance. He later claimed he collected enough spent cannonballs to pay for any damage sustained by the village. The Americans had a twelve-pound cannon at Parish's dock, a brass six-pound cannon that could be moved wherever needed and about 1,200 men stationed on the west side of the Oswegatchie River, awaiting a possible attack. Using David Parish's telescope the next morning, General Brown watched as the Canadian and British forces at Prescott prepared for an attack.[83]

The attack was not long in coming. On Sunday, October 4, the somewhat rash and ineffective British colonel Robert Lethbridge led a force of about seven hundred[84] men in twenty-five boats accompanied by two gunboats and headed upriver with the apparent intent of floating back downstream to attack Ogdensburg. However, the Americans were ready for them when they came, and by the time they got within one thousand feet of the American shore, the British were showered with a withering fire from the militia and regulars stationed on both sides of the Oswegatchie. Daniel Church manned the brass six-pounder at the wooden battery near the Parish store, while Sheriff Joseph York and his volunteers manned the twelve-pounder. When the twelve-pound cannon was fired, it recoiled downhill, and Sheriff York could not get it back up into position, so Church sent some of his men to help. Once back into position, York began firing grape shot to great effect, but there was no grape shot that would fit the Church's brass cannon, so he stuck with the round shot available to him. The Canadians and British were sitting ducks and quickly realized that they could not produce enough effective fire to cover their landing as they bobbed around in the water. The closer they got to shore, the more lopsided the battle became, with the American troops safely hidden behind buildings and ramparts while the British sat in open boats.

The only wise decision Lethbridge made that entire day was the decision to call off the attack. The force rowed post-haste for the safety of their own waters, having had one boat badly damaged and losing two men.[85] Colonel Lethbridge never commanded again in the St. Lawrence valley, as he was replaced by the much more capable Lieutenant Colonel Thomas Pearson. In *Reminiscences of Ogdensburg*, Daniel Church is quoted as saying that subsequent newspaper accounts of the skirmish (referring to the October 6, 1812 *Palladium*) mentioned soldiers who hid behind Parish's stone store but did not mention him or his crew, who valiantly faced the enemy in the open.[86] The Americans suffered no casualties, but there was some damage to some of the houses in town. General Brown told Nathan Ford that he believed the British were trying to entice the gunboat *Dolphin* out of its berth to try and capture it—and the *Dolphin* did set sail, but it was immediately ordered back to port.

Governor Tompkins realized the situation at Ogdensburg was precarious, but he had few options. The New York militia there had been federalized, so he no longer had control of them. He therefore wrote to General Dodge at Sackets Harbor and asked that he send the remainder of Forsyth's men, plus whatever militia he could spare, to Ogdensburg as soon as possible. These reinforcements arrived there on October 12, 1812.[87]

The aborted invasion of October 4 and the constant threat of another, perhaps more intelligent one, convinced General Brown to augment the defenses of Ogdensburg. Therefore, on November 5, 1812, men under his command began to build a redoubt to be known as Fort Oswegatchie at the downriver end of the village near the slaughterhouse. The militia supplied the labor, but Joseph Jacques Ramee, who was in town designing the interior of David Parish's mansion, supplied the design.[88]

Fort Rensselaer, on the west side of the Oswegatchie, received its baptism of fire just a few days later. At about 1:00 a.m. on November 17, 1812, three or four British gunboats approached the American shore about one mile above Ogdensburg. An American sentry hailed them, and they began to fire at the hapless fellow. He was soon joined by other riflemen, and the boats made off, but not without first firing several ineffective shots at Fort Rensselaer. The six-pounder emplaced on the point returned the fire, and no real damage was done to either side, although David Parish was narrowly missed.[89]

By this time, it was obvious to Forsyth and any other observer that the people of the Ogdensburg area were, at best, lukewarm to the war fever. They continued to trade with the Canadians and hoped the whole war situation would die down and go away. Louis Hasbrouck, the county clerk, somewhat optimistically put it in a letter dated November 20, 1812, that "there is considerable buzz about peace,"[90] but he was deluding himself and had yet to understand the mindset of Captain Benjamin Forsyth, who was itching for a fight.

Toward the end of November, Forsyth wrote again to the War Department, practically begging for the winter clothing he had asked for months ago. He had personally paid for 125 pairs of shoes for his men by borrowing money and confessed that he had no more of his own money with which to purchase needed clothing. He mentioned that by continuing enlistments, he had increased his command to 151 effectives and was in desperate need of an ensign to help him run the outfit.[91]

The next demonstration of Forsyth's aggressiveness occurred on November 26, 1812. He had sent some men in a boat upriver in search for firewood, since five months of militia occupation had effectively stripped the surrounding countryside of anything remotely flammable, including trees, bushes, driftwood and the occasional board fence. Two or three British gunboats saw them in an exposed position and attacked them with grape shot. Forsyth grabbed twelve of his men, jumped into a boat and rowed to within rifle distance of them and shot accurately enough to convince the British of the error of their ways. At this point in time, there were several British gunboats stationed at Prescott, and they did all the harassment. A newspaper account stated that the batteries on shore at Prescott had not fired on Ogdensburg since the attack of October 4.[92]

An account of the November 26 firewood skirmish appeared in the *New York Herald* on December 15, 1812, and included a report of an exchange between some of Forsyth's officers concerning their opinion of the local citizens. It was occasioned by the fairly common practice of allowing the British to come to Ogdensburg under a flag of truce to visit and for trading, an unusual situation between combatants in any "normal" conflict. One American officer is supposed to have said, "I believe it is owing to some of the inhabitants of this village that there are so many flags sent over, and I'll be damned if I don't wish one third of them were massacred." Another officer is said to have declaimed against the Peace Party: "I wish all who speak against the administration of government were stretched by the neck." The writer adds that the patriotism of the residents of Ogdensburg was above reproach and that since the identity of the first officer is known, he will be watched as vigilantly "as the villain who stabs in the dark." And as for the comments about the Peace Party, they were made by a "violent politician who is considered no better than a talking mule who merely echoes the sentiments of those who lead him by the nose."

At Christmas 1812, the six-month draft period of the militia expired, and most of the men went home. A few stayed on, as did all of Forsyth's men, who were still living in Nathan Ford's old garrison on the west side of the Oswegatchie. Captain John Lytle of Lisbon also enlisted a company of one-year men for duty at Ogdensburg, and these men were ultimately attached to Forsyth's command. Joshua Conkey of Canton enlisted about twenty-five men to act as artillerymen for a period of three months, and there were probably a few other militiamen who elected to stay on a while longer, including Captain Giles Kellogg and a few of his Schoharie County men. Even the senior officers went home and back to their families, as General Jacob Brown asked for and received permission from Governor Tompkins to let Captain Forsyth act as the local commander while he returned to Brownville in Jefferson County.[93]

It is interesting to note that at the end of December 1812, Lieutenant Colonel Pearson wrote to Sir George Prevost telling him that although it would not be difficult to attack and capture Ogdensburg, it would not be worth it overall, since he thought it would "rouse all the country to retaliate" against Prescott. He suggested waiting until the weather was more favorable, as they would also be able to capture the two American armed schooners that were frozen in the ice at the time.[94]

Lieutenant Colonel Thomas B. Benedict had moved to Ogdensburg for the period of the militia activation and wanted to continue on in state or federal service. He wrote to Governor Daniel Tompkins on November 21, 1812, apparently asking that the militia be federalized, and presumably, with him at the head. Tompkins replied three weeks later that it was not in his power to federalize the militia until Madison or some other federal official requested it. Interestingly, Benedict must have also inquired about members of the local populace slandering him to the governor. Tompkins answered that he had nothing to worry about and that the efforts of Judge Ford and others to undermine him would come to naught. He assured Benedict that if he had any concerns about him, "I shall not hesitate to communicate it directly to you or your general in black and white."[95] Benedict also tried to get a commission in the regular army, but with no success. On February 2, 1813, he wrote to David Parish at his home in Philadelphia asking for his intercession with the secretary of war, but again to no effect.[96] Later in the month, he traveled to Albany to try and get reimbursed for the money he had personally spent on furnishing the militia with blankets, cooking utensils, etc.

Since the six-month drafted men had been discharged in December, Governor Tompkins authorized a new draft of 5,000 men for the 1813 campaign. Resistance to the war was just as strong as ever in heavily Federalist St. Lawrence County. Roswell Hopkins of Hopkinton, who was assemblyman for the county, reported that men "in every town I have heard from have manifested a determination to resist" the draft. Only 1,500 of the 5,000 men actually reported for duty.[97] Michael Seabury of Massena, who was related to Captain David Sheik of Sheik's Island in Massena, passed information on to the British commander in Cornwall from time to time. Seabury related several stories, including one in which a Waddington resident named Monk (perhaps George Monk, 1797–1858) got himself "captured" by the Canadians and paroled so that he could not be drafted into the militia.

Other minor skirmishes occurred from time to time, as would be expected when two armed forces are separated by a distance of only a mile. For example, the February 2, 1813 *New York Herald* published an account of seven men from Captain Kellogg's volunteer artillery approaching within seventy yards of the Canadian shore on January 15, drawing fire from the pickets posted there. Forsyth, who had been promoted to major on January 20, dispatched Lieutenant William C. Baird with forty men to rescue their comrades, resulting in the withdrawal of the Canadians. The paper makes a point of stating that the original incursion by the artillerymen was not sanctioned by Forsyth.

But Benjamin Forsyth was no armchair soldier. He liked nothing better than to mix it up, especially when he had the advantage of surprise. Case in point: the raid on Elizabethtown[98] (now called Brockville) on the night of February 6, 1813. It should be remembered that the British were faced with several disadvantages during the war that they could not ameliorate. One was the sparse population of the Canadas, which meant that there were fewer farms and thus fewer homegrown provisions for British troops. This forced the importation of much of the foodstuffs, livestock and other items necessary for the support of any military force. Another inherent disadvantage they had was the simple fact that a large majority of that sparse population was transplanted Americans. Although these Loyalists may have had little affection for America, they had even less affection for the British monarch but were drawn northward by the allure of cheap, plentiful land. As a result, when the British needed to rely on militia to defend the border, many of the military-aged men had no appetite for fighting their erstwhile countrymen. Draft evasion and desertion were serious problems on both sides of the border, especially in the summer, when there was fieldwork to do on the farms.

Major Forsyth heard that a party of British had crossed the river on February 4, 1813, and captured some prisoners,[99] some of whom may have been pickets on patrol, and some of whom may have been Canadian draft evaders. It appears that some of these formerly American draft resisters/deserters were held in the jail at Elizabethtown, and reports came across the porous border concerning their plight. Sympathy for anyone unwilling to serve the British king inspired Forsyth to formulate a plan for their release. Therefore, on the night of February 6, 1813, he loaded about two hundred men, including some of his own men and some of Captain John Lytle's, into sleighs and set off for Morristown, directly across the river from Elizabethtown. Even Colonel Benedict volunteered for the expedition. At Morristown, he enlisted the services of innkeeper Arnold Smith, who knew the layout of the settlement across the river. They crossed the river in two divisions, Forsyth at the head of one and Benedict leading the other, with flanking details up and down river commanded by Lieutenant George R. Wells and Lieutenant Johnson. These flanking detachments were to be posted at each end of the village to prevent the summoning of assistance. Forsyth himself personally attacked the jail, freeing sixteen prisoners, while his men attacked the sleeping garrison. An accused murderer named Edward McSween (or McSwiney) was the only other denizen of the jail, and he was not liberated in spite of his pleas to Forsyth. Major Bartholomew Carley; Captains Jones, Steward and Hubbell; and forty-six privates of the First and Second Leeds Rifle Companies were captured and brought back to Ogdensburg, where they were paroled. Forsyth also captured 120 stands of arms that had been lost by the Americans at Detroit, as well as two casks of powder.

This audacious raid was almost undoubtedly the reason that his subsequent promotion to brevet lieutenant colonel was backdated to February 6, 1813, but as Nathan Ford so presciently wrote to his brother on February 18, "The folly and mischief this may produce can only be anticipated." He was not alone in his analysis of the result. Quoting the Herkimer *American*, the March 2, 1813 *Northern Whig* wrote:

> *This enterprise of Capt. Forsyth, although resulting in success, is considered by many inhabitants on the St. Lawrence as extremely prejudicial to the settlements of that new country, and perhaps induce others to remove to places of greater safety than are to be found on an extensive and exposed frontier, where our own troops are setting an example of predatory excursions into the enemy's territory, which may be visited up on ourselves a thousand-fold to our disadvantage. It is much to be lamented that some of our military commanders hold and practice on this maxim: That while the nation is at war, the people shall not have peace.*[100]

Note that one man's "daring rescue" is another man's "predatory excursion." Others also noted the attack on Brockville and the renewed activity at the fort in Prescott. Joseph Rosseel wrote to Parish, "Our wizards prophecy an attack on this place…the militia of this town is again called up."[101]

A week later, some of Forsyth's men, including Lieutenant William C. Baird, raided across the river and captured three farmers and a team of horses. There is no further mention of the farmers in local records, but Colonel Pearson sent a flag over to Captain Forsyth in the person of thirty-one-year-old Major George "Red George" MacDonell, second in command at Prescott, demanding the surrender of the horses and stating Pearson's threat that for every horse taken, he would send his Indians over to take a scalp. Forsyth, in his typically diplomatic tone, told him they could "come over and be damned."[102] It was apparently during this conversation that Forsyth also made an offer of meeting Pearson on the ice in person, where they could have it out man-to-man. MacDonell is reported to have replied that he would be in charge at Prescott soon and would have no objections to granting Forsyth's wish.[103]

Another point of mutual irritation at this time was the habit of criminals from both sides of the river breaking out of jail and escaping to the other shore, with the civil authorities from both sides demanding the return of the prisoners, even though most of them would certainly have made as much distance as they could between themselves and the local courts. John Ross mentions a somewhat amusing example of this phenomenon:

> *The great vagabond who is suspected of murdering the woman at Potsdam and who was, by the last court, for other crimes condemned to 14 years imprisonment in the USP, has, with another culprit, got safe out of his confinement in our Courthouse in the night from Thursday to Friday, and as we now know, re-visited our Canadian neighbors. When he was confined, Sheriff Davies said if he escaped from his care, he would allow himself to be hung in his place. I do not know if he now means to act up to it.*[104]

During all this excitement and the occasional raid to steal horses, the British were hardly idle. The fort at the eastern edge of Prescott was actively engaged in improving its offensive capabilities. Joseph Rosseel saw the increasing prowess at Prescott through rose-colored glasses when he said, "Additional batteries at Prescott is another indication of their disposition to act altogether on the defensive. But we stand a chance of being shot by ours—a random bullet came very near striking Edward near the house of Mr. Ross."[105]

With little to show after eight months of hostilities, the federal government was having more and more trouble recruiting men for the U.S. Army. The pay was low, and even the enticement of free land was not enough to fill their enlistment quotas. Physically, recruits were supposed to be free from sore legs, scurvy, scalled head, ruptures and other infirmities. There was no height requirement, but he had to be strong, active and healthy. The minimum age was eighteen, but healthy boys from thirteen to eighteen could enlist as musicians with the consent of a parent, guardian or master.[106]

As so often seemed to be the case, Nathan Ford seemed almost clairvoyant sometimes when dealing with people he considered scoundrels and fools. He had gone to Albany for political meetings and wrote to his brother David from there on February 18, 1813, "[I shall] return by Sackets Harbor. My object in this is to have a conference with Col. McComb for the purpose of restraining Capt. Forsyth in his Canada excursions. I fear he will lead us into some cursed scrape. I think if something is not done, he will land us in a broil that will not be easily laid by." He would be proved correct just one hundred hours later.

Chapter 4

THE LION SCRATCHES BACK

When distilled to its essentials, history is really just a study of how events, sometimes seemingly unconnected, are in reality links in the same long chain. So how the sick leave of a middle-aged man in Toronto led to the death of a nineteen-year-old boy from Canton is one of the underlying stories of the Battle of Ogdensburg.

Sir George Prevost, the governor-in-chief of British North America, was in Quebec City in February 1813 attending the Seventh Parliament of Lower Canada, which he prorogued on the seventeenth of that month. Soon after, he headed up the St. Lawrence River valley, intending to visit Montreal, Prescott, Kingston and, ultimately, York, the provincial capital of Upper Canada. Along the way, he undoubtedly met with local civic and military leaders, as he was also a lieutenant general and supreme commander of the British forces in Canada. His party, including deputy adjutant general Lieutenant Colonel Sir John Harvey, stopped in Prescott on the afternoon of February 21, 1813, to pick up Colonel Pearson and take him to Kingston so that he could be in charge of that place in the absence of Colonel John Vincent. Colonel Vincent was himself being temporarily reassigned to York (Toronto) in order to fill in for the ailing Major General Roger Sheaffe, who happened to be Pearson's brother-in-law.[107]

Prevost and his escort stayed overnight in Prescott, Prevost taking over the wooden commanding officer's quarters, which was part of the commissariat of stores. The plan was to make the sixty-mile trip to Kingston in two hard days of sleighing. Prevost, Pearson and their respective entourages left

Prescott in sleighs before the sun came up on February 22, 1813, guarded by a detail of Indians commanded by twenty-six-year-old Captain Robert P. Skinner of the Royal Newfoundland Regiment. The fact that two men had deserted from Prescott during the night added a certain urgency to Prevost's departure, on the assumption that the deserters would have almost certainly informed the Ogdensburg garrison of the presence of a very high-value target about to head up to Kingston.

Colonel Pearson had been given fairly explicit instructions to refrain from fighting with the Americans, but he had no qualms about MacDonell making a noisy "demonstration" on the ice to distract the Americans and cover Prevost's departure. MacDonell also made the case that if he drew out the Americans from their barracks, he could judge whether they had already sent a party upriver to lay in waiting for Prevost's convoy of sleighs. Although ordered not to attack, there is an old saying in the military that "it's easier to get forgiveness than it is to get permission," so by the time Pearson and Prevost had gotten out of earshot, Major MacDonell was leading the attack on Ogdensburg.

For at least a month or so, the British had been noisily drilling and parading each morning before breakfast, first on the parade ground east of the village, and, once the river froze solidly, on the thick ice of the St. Lawrence. These daily exercises, run by Lieutenant George Ridge, the staff adjutant, had inured the American sentries to the sight and sounds of large formations of troops marching and drilling in the pre-dawn haze only two thousand yards away. However, on this particular day, this was no drill. MacDonell had roughly seven hundred effectives at his disposal that morning, a mixture of regulars and militia, and he was very well aware of how lightly Ogdensburg was defended, with just a few militia and Forsyth's regulars. He divided his force into two groups. A small detachment on the right flank would get around the point where the garrison sat and cut off any escape attempt, while the main body of men on the left would attack the village itself, sweep through the American defenses and gain control of the bridge over the Oswegatchie so that they could finish off Forsyth once and for all.

The right flank was led by Captain John Jenkins and consisted of the Right Flank Company of the Glengarry Light Fencibles and about seventy men who were part of companies from Glengarry County and Dundas County militias commanded by Alexander Macmillan and Michael Ault, respectively. Also attached to this column were two Royal Artillerymen pulling a six-pound cannon mounted on a sled.

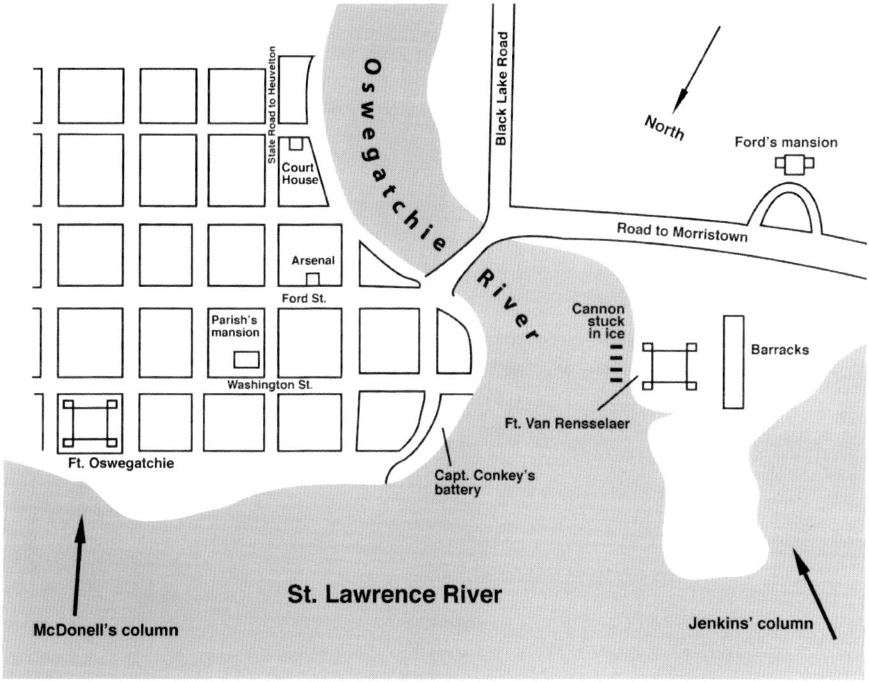

Battle of Ogdensburg as seen from the attackers' point of view.

MacDonell himself commanded the larger, left wing of attack, and he was aided by Colonel Thomas Fraser. MacDonell had about 400 men, including 120 from the Eighth Regiment of Foot, a few from the Forty-first Welsh Regiment and 30 or so Royal Newfoundlanders. About 230 Canadian militiamen rounded out his force. MacDonell signaled the attack by firing a gun, and once the two columns were in motion, there was no turning back and no time to lose. The average man can cover a mile in fifteen minutes under normal conditions, but slogging across snow-covered ice while weighed down with heavy winter coats and all the accoutrements of war could not be considered normal conditions. And although the Americans would sooner or later realize what was happening, time was of the essence. Legend has it that Forsyth was shaving when word got to him that the British would be his guests for breakfast in a matter of minutes.

Captain Jenkins's men had a slightly farther run ahead of them, trying to gain the point and come around the west side of it before coming on shore. However, by the time they got directly in front of the point, the game was up, and the American artillery near the garrison fired on them, killing one of the two Royal Artillerymen.

One obstacle faced by both columns faced that they had not counted on was the depth of the snowdrifts as they got closer to shore. Their long garrison coats became even more of a hindrance as they struggled to keep from falling into the snow. Captain Jenkins and his men were in combat first because of their nearness to the fort. Jenkins was at the very head of his column, yelling and waving his pistol in encouragement. They got within charging distance of the garrison and fixed bayonets, completely out of breath from their six-thousand-foot dash. As Jenkins struggled in the snow and raised his left arm to keep his balance, it was struck by grape shot from one of the five cannons stationed near the fort and was nearly blown completely off his body. The concussion dropped him to the now-crimson ice, but he managed to get back on his feet and again strove to rally his men. He was able to take a few steps, but within seconds, his other arm was also struck, and he went down. This time, the shock and loss of blood made it impossible for him to stand. Some of his men pressed on without him, however, and a majority of these raw troops retreated in disarray all the way back to Prescott, carrying their dead and wounded. Once back on the other side, they were basically forced to return to the fight a few minutes later by the exhortations and threats of bodily harm emitted by the six-foot-four Bishop Alexander MacDonell.

At the other end of the village, MacDonell's force initially had a much easier time of it. Few militiamen were on station in that part of the village, and the guns of the garrison were preoccupied with Jenkins and his men. The as-yet-unfinished Fort Oswegatchie was not occupied, but it is probable that the two-gun battery at the foot of Caroline Street was manned, at least initially. MacDonell's men waded through the drifts and came onshore near the battery and then swung around to the left to ensure that Fort Oswegatchie would pose no threat to their advance. One aspect of the attack that should be taken into account is the fact that the British officers (and presumably many of the enlisted men) had been in Ogdensburg many times visiting and shopping at Rosseel's store, so they had an intimate knowledge of the village and knew which streets went where. They then split into several columns and made their way to Ford Street,[108] the principal thoroughfare of the village, which would lead them to the bridge over the Oswegatchie—and to Forsyth and his command. Although MacDonell's column included several cannons, they were too far in the rear of the action to be of any service to him at first. The river current and overnight winds had produced a tangle of broken ledges of ice and deep snowdrifts on the shore that the artillerymen struggled against for many precious minutes. Even a six-pound cannon weighs enough that pulling it uphill is an exhausting task.

MacDonell needed those cannons to get into position at the end of Washington Street so that they could soften up Forsyth's defenses, but the gunners were doing their best and were exhausted after their cross-river jaunt. The advance guard of MacDonell's column, which was made up of the Newfoundland men and some militia, spied the sled-mounted twelve-pound cannon of Captain Joshua Conkey's artillery not far from Parish's stone store, which was manned but had not yet fired a shot. The advanced guard charged Conkey's position, while the main body flanked them on the left and forced them to surrender before they could fire a single round. They quickly got the prisoners out of the way and set about turning the American gun on the old fort.

Some of the American militia who had been dislodged from their positions began a harassing fire, falling back toward the center of town and shooting from behind houses and trees, so small details of British were sent to silence their guns. Meanwhile, part of the invading force reached Ford Street and headed down toward the bridge but were greeted by the iron twelve-pounder[109] of Captain Giles Kellogg's men set up on the corner of Euphemia (now State) and Ford Streets and a single brass six-pounder a little farther down toward the bridge. This smaller cannon was manned by Sheriff Joseph York and two assistant gunners.

With nearly one thousand men involved in the battle altogether, there would be nearly one thousand different stories of heroism, luck and cowardice. Almost all those stories are untold today, but two have come down to us through the last two centuries.

Sheriff Joseph York (who was replaced as sheriff two months later by Thomas J. Davies) and some volunteers manned the cannon in the center of the block on Ford Street between Euphemia and Isabela Streets, guarding the bridge across the Oswegatchie. Assuming that any attack would be on the west side of the river, their cannons were facing across the Oswegatchie, protecting the bridge. When they discovered that the main body of the British troops was advancing on them from behind, they had to quickly try to wheel the cannons around and fire at their attackers coming at them down Ford Street. Aiming, loading and firing a cannon takes time, and as each second passed, the British got closer, and their musket fire got more accurate. Kellogg's men got one shot off but could not adjust their aim because the cannon's elevating screw snapped off. They decided it would be prudent to

View of the north side of Parish's mansion, showing the stone wall facing Washington Street, which bore the marks of British musket and cannon fire. *Courtesy of the St. Lawrence County Historical Association.*

abandon the post and ran past York and across the bridge to the relative safety of the old fort, abandoning their cannon to the onrushing British.

Kellogg's retreat left York and his men to face the entire attacking column by themselves. The British took up the full width of Ford Street and were several rows deep, coming at York at a dead run. York got off one shot, right down the middle of the road, and the front line of troops reflexively dove into the snow trying to save their skins, but somebody in the rear rank almost certainly was wounded. The British then reloaded their muskets, got back on their feet and continued the charge. Two of York's assistants, Joseph Kneeland and a Mr. Hyde, were both killed as they helped load the cannon, but York remained unscathed and got off at least one more shot. However, troops can run faster than a man can load a cannon by himself, and York was soon overpowered. Legend has it that he was about to be done in when Captain Eustace of the King's Regiment told his troops to spare his life, as he was too brave a man to kill. He was captured and paroled later, partly due to the exertions of his wife to win his freedom.

Another unsung hero of that day was Salmon Jones of Canton, a nineteen-year-old artilleryman who escaped being captured when Captain Joshua

Conkey's company surrendered. There was an old store on the south side of Ford Street between State and Isabella Streets, just past York's position, that was used as an arsenal at that time. It is not clear why an arsenal was located in the village instead of at the old garrison, but for some reason, it was. Jones got to the arsenal and began firing down Ford Street toward the charging British. He apparently killed at least one enemy soldier but was attacked and either shot once or bayoneted to death as he held out the position by himself. This is how, as mentioned before, the sick leave of a middle-aged man in Toronto (General Sheaffe) caused a shift in British commanders that occasioned the attack on Ogdensburg in which nineteen-year-old Salmon Jones lost his life.

Elements of the American militia ran farther into the village, and some kept running, but others took cover in or behind buildings and put up a harassing fire. Many of those who did not run away into the woods crossed the bridge over the Oswegatchie and headed to the relative safety of Forsyth's firepower.

Once the high ground near the bridge was taken, MacDonell decided to call a halt to regroup. His men were completely played out from the one-mile run across the ice and their struggle through the deep drifts to climb up onto the shore. He also needed time for his men to turn around the overrun cannon of Captain Conkey's artillery and get it in place for the bombardment of the fort. MacDonell must have been pleased with events so far: he was in command of the entire village except for perhaps a few snipers, and at least so far, his casualties had been minimal. He decided to see if he could complete his conquest the easy way.

Dan Church and Lieutenant William Baird from Forsyth's company were in front of the barracks about to fire their six-pounders at MacDonell's position when a white flag of truce borne by Canadians Duncan Fraser and Jonas Jones appeared near the bridge. The two officers crossed over and advised Forsyth to surrender or face a death by bayonet. Forsyth's reply that there was "still fighting left to be done" could not have been much of a surprise to MacDonell, who probably would have answered the same if the roles had been reversed.

The British control of the east bank of the Oswegatchie—and effectively the entire town—put Forsyth in the unenviable position of fighting ahead of him and in his rear at the same time. One can only imagine the noise, the confusion, the clouds of gun smoke, the concussion of the cannon and the blood spattered all over the snow. But the fight did continue, with Forsyth losing several valuable men because of wounds, including Adjutant Dan

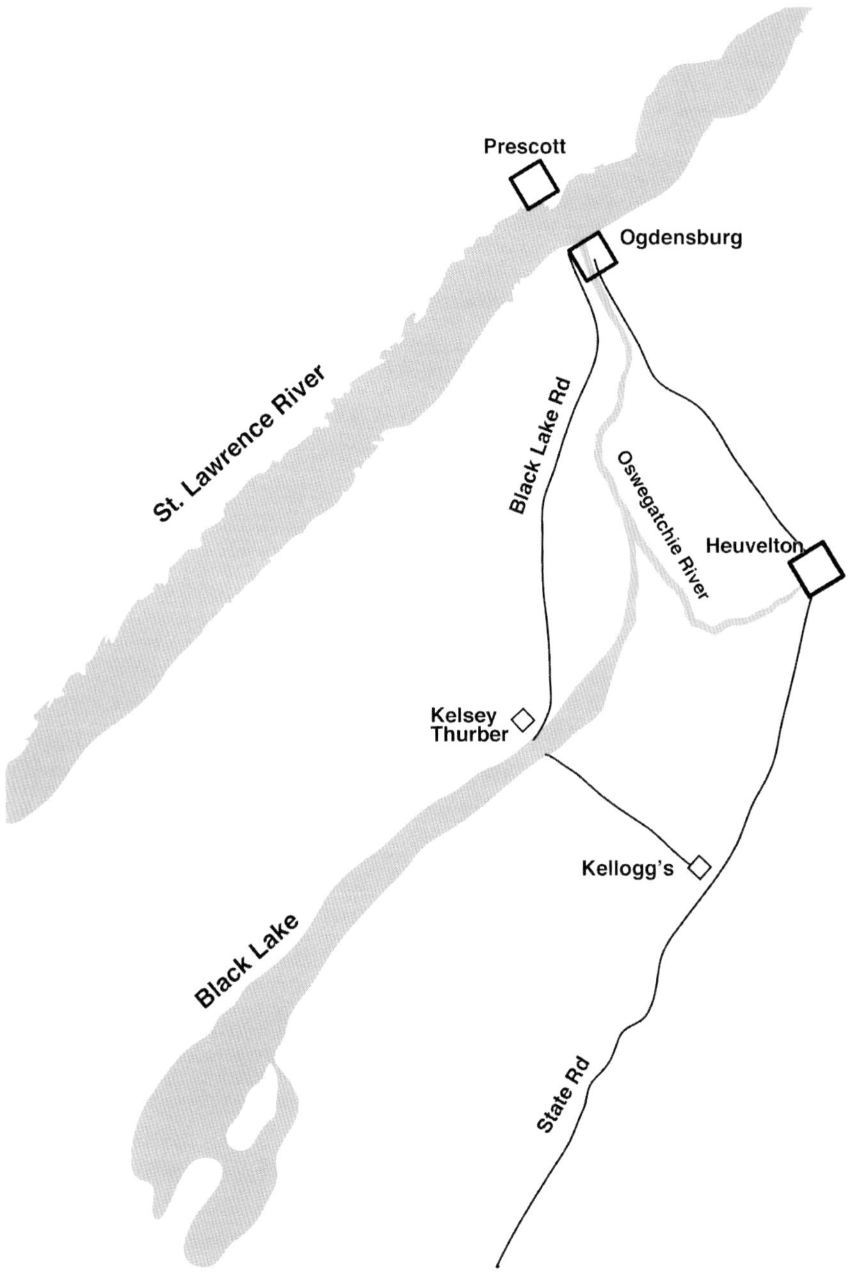

Routes of the American escape out of Ogdensburg.

Church, who was wounded in the groin by grape shot, and Lieutenant Baird, who was seriously wounded in the foot.

In a sense, Forsyth had lived for this moment, but he was not suicidal, and he ultimately saw that his position was untenable. He was obviously outnumbered by the British and was being fired upon not just by the infantry but also by the British and captured American cannons. Although defending a peninsula sometimes has its advantages, it always has the disadvantage of leaving only one route of escape by land. The remnants of Jenkins's column were behind them and getting closer every minute, so Forsyth gave the order to retreat before their only escape route could be cut off by MacDonell. He and his men fled down what is now called New York Avenue and did not stop until they reached Kelsey Thurber's house on the north shore of Black Lake. From there, they cut across the frozen lake and went cross-country to Kellogg's place at the corner of the State Road (now County Route 10) and what is now County Route 11 just a mile southwest of Depeyster. The wounded Daniel Church was able to make good his escape, but Lieutenant Baird was hurt badly enough that he could not walk and so was left at Nathan Ford's mansion as the men hurried out of town. He was captured and sent to Montreal.

The remaining militia on the east side of the river saw Forsyth make his exit. Because the British stood between them and the Oswegatchie, those survivors of Conkey and Kellogg's artillery and John Lytle's volunteers who were not captured, along with several other militia stragglers, could not join Forsyth's men and so escaped out of the village by running down State Street without stopping until they got to Jairus Remington's tavern in Heuvelton, six miles away. Except for a few parting musket shots, the British forces did not pursue either group, as a few extra prisoners were more of a burden than a prize. What they were interested in was the large amount of food and materials stored there at Ogdensburg for the use of the army. There were tents, blankets, barrels of pork, whiskey, ammunition, cannons, hundreds of muskets and various other items that were far more valuable than a few prisoners.

It was at about this point in the capture of the town that an almost comical incident took place. Captain Skinner, who until an hour earlier had been leading the Indians as they escorted Prevost to Kingston, rode into Ogdensburg with an express message for MacDonell. It was from Prevost himself, who had written it at 9:00 a.m. as he and his party got to Flint's Tavern near Brockville for breakfast. MacDonell must have laughed out loud as he read it:

An 1830s sketch of Parish's store. The ruins of Fort Van Rensselaer can be seen across the river on the left. *Courtesy St. Lawrence University Special Collections.*

> *You will not undertake any offensive operations against Ogdensburgh without previous communication with Major-General de Rottenburg, unless imbecile conduct of your enemy should offer you an opportunity for his destruction…nor do I think it proper to beget irritation in the mind of the people of the United States by any act that does not bear on the face of it a just retaliation on the military forces of that country for wanton and unprovoked injury.*[110]

Sometimes, one man's good luck is connected to another's bad luck. A case in point is William Hollenbeck of Canton, who volunteered to be a member of Joshua Conkey's artillery company. Some sort of family emergency made him hire a substitute for a few weeks to cover his absence so that he could be at home during much of January 1813. The substitute, Thomas Conkey, son of the commander, served in his place until February 21, the day Hollenbeck returned for duty at Ogdensburg. Conkey left Ogdensburg and was safe at home when Hollenbeck was captured by the British.

The British captured all the armaments abandoned at the old barracks, as well as all the cannons, ammunition, flour, pork, beef, tallow, butter and whiskey. They also took the time to free two iron cannons and a brass nine-pounder that were frozen in the ice on the shore near the garrison. Although not listed in the official records, Forsyth's sword, which he had hastily left in his quarters, was captured and has been on display at Prescott for two hundred years.

According to the *Kingston Gazette*, the British casualties were:

> *Royal Artillery: 1 rank and file killed*
> *King's Regt.: 1 sergeant killed, 12 rank and file wounded*
> *Newfoundland Regt.: 1 rank and file killed, 4 rank and file wounded*
> *Glengarry Light Infantry: 2 rank and file killed, 1 Lt. Col., 1 Capt, 1 Lieut. 2 sergeants and 7 rank and file wounded*
> *Militia: 2 rank and file killed, 1 captain, 3 subalterns, 1 sergeant 15 rank and file wounded*[111]

It was at Kellogg's place in modern-day Depeyster that Joseph Rosseel found Forsyth (whose hat and coat were pierced with bullet holes) and some of his Ogdensburg friends,[112] including the wounded Daniel W. Church, who had arrived there in Forsyth's sleigh. Church later got a sleigh to take him to Remington's tavern in Heuvelton, where Mrs. Remington treated his wound. The next morning, General Brown came through with some militia from Sackets Harbor, hoping to salvage some of the military stores in Ogdensburg. Brown met Church at Heuvelton and offered to take him back to Ogdensburg in his sleigh. Church relates that when he got to Ogdensburg, there were British officers there rifling through a building, and he gave them his opinion of them in no uncertain terms being "gifted like a Methodist preacher."[113] Louis Hasbrouck wrote to his wife the next month and said that none of the residents of Ogdensburg were killed or wounded but that a soldier's child had been killed in Ichabod Tuttle's house when a musket ball passed through.

Besides the loss of life, the invaders inflicted other damage as well. They burned the old and new barracks of the old garrison; burned the schooners *Niagara* and *Dolphin* (one belonging to Joseph Rosseel and Co., and another belonging to the government), which were frozen in the harbor, also burning two gunboats which were likewise frozen in the harbor; and destroyed the guard houses. They also tried to burn the bridge over the Oswegatchie but

Joseph Rosseel's home, now the site of the Ogdensburg Library. *Courtesy of the St. Lawrence County Historical Association.*

were only partially successful due to the amount of ice and snow built up on it.[114] They even opened the jail, freeing a man named Bigelow and one other, perhaps in retaliation for Forsyth's opening the jail in Elizabethtown a few weeks earlier.

Adding insult to injury, many Canadian civilians, including women, came over to plunder private homes, several of which were unoccupied due to the longstanding threat of attack. Daniel Church stated that only three houses were unmolested: those of David Parish, John Scott and one other he left unnamed but was certainly the mansion of Nathan Ford, who was in Utica at the time.[115] First Sergeant Rogers of Forsyth's company later told William Hollenbeck that he was ordered to hide all Forsyth's regimental paperwork in the cellar of Judge Ford's mansion. However, the British searched the house and found the documents but did not disturb any of Ford's possessions, which later led to whispers of treachery.[116] Although not ransacked, Parish's mansion suffered somewhat just by its nearness to the action. Not a single window in the house escaped without at least one pane of glass being shattered by the artillery concussions, and the fence around his home was riddled with shot and shell fragments. Louis Hasbrouck's house, closer to the river than Parish's, suffered a similar fate, as did Andrew McCollom's house on the corner of Ford and Euphemia.[117]

Approximately sixty prisoners were taken, including Major Watson, Bemsley Huntoon and Sheriff York, who, along with other non-combatants, were released on parole. Joseph Rosseel was in the process of being captured when a British officer, an acquaintance of Rosseel's, happened by and had him released. Those captives who were under arms were sent to Johnstown, a short distance downriver from Prescott, then to Montreal (where a few later escaped) and, ultimately, Halifax and England. Colonel MacDonell told Rosseel that if he ever heard that there were more than fifty to one hundred men stationed in Ogdensburg (enough to guard against pillaging), he would burn Ogdensburg to the ground.[118] As noted by historian Benson J. Lossing, the Americans suffered five killed and fifteen wounded, while the British suffered six killed and forty-eight wounded British—a rather somber way to celebrate Washington's birthday.

One would think that after having been attacked and having their village ransacked, there would have been a popular uprising against the British foe. Although some harbored hate and resentment, it appears that the majority of the inhabitants agreed with the sentiments of the writer (perhaps Ford himself) below:

> *I wrote you a hasty letter by the last post in which I told you I would give you a circumstantial account of the attack upon Ogdensburgh together with the causes which led to it. This event has been produced by our own folly, or rather by the folly of the commandant, which heightens the mortification produced by this untoward affair. The commandant, Capt. Forsyth, is a soldier of bravery and is an excellent partisan officer but in my judgment lacks those qualifications which constitute an able commandant of a post situate as Ogdensburgh was. His zeal to signalize himself absorbs all other considerations, and although a man of good sense, he has suffered his prejudices to govern instead of his better judgment. He ought to have observed that neither the administration or Gen. Dearborn were taking measures to replace an adequate force after the time of service of the militia under Gen. Brown had expired, which was the 26th of December last.*
>
> *Col. McDonald has conducted with great humanity and liberality towards the people of Ogdensburgh. He did, as far as possible, prevent plundering, but it was out of his power totally to prevent it. Many of the villagers were totally stripped and few escaped the effects which a scene like this was calculated to produce. Col. Macdonald has assured the inhabitants*

every exertion shall be made to restore the property plundered. A number of yoke of oxen have been returned, also a number of horses, and he is doing all he can do to recover the other property. He requested a statement might be made of the property lost which was done by a committee of the villagers and yesterday they waited upon the Colonel with it when he assured them he would use every exertion to restore the property. A valuation was made out which he assured the committee he would lay before Gov. Provost on his return from York.

There was a considerable quantity of provisions taken from individuals which he says shall be paid for, and I make no doubt great liberality will be extended to those who have lost other property and they, I hope, will be remunerated in part, if not in whole. There is no British soldiers in the village, or any suffered to come except with a flag accompanied with an officer. The handsome conduct of Col. M'Donald satisfies us we shall receive no insult.

We are, as you may suppose, in a disagreeable situation when we have to appeal to the clemency of our enemy instead of receiving protection from our government. The property burnt were the barracks at the northeast of the village, the old garrison, the blockhouse in Fort Van Rensselaer, a schooner in the harbor, and such boats as were full of ice and snow. The public property taken I am not able to detail; it however, was very considerable. Among it were about 1,000 stand of arms, with equipments complete, a great number of tents, a large quantity of ammunition, very considerable magazines of provision etc. also 2 long 12 pounders, 2 double fortified 9's, 2 brass 9's 2 brass 6's, 2 iron 4's, and one other, 11 in all. This immense property was sent to the lines, within cannon shot of the British garrison, and our wise men which supposed the troops which were idling in Greenbush were nigh enough to protect it. But this is of a piece with the rest of their management. I admit consistency is a good thing, and our wise men have a great share of it. Governor Tompkins and Gen. Dearborn have long since and repeatedly been informed of the situation of this…and I consider the present disaster chargeable upon them. But Gen. Dearborn more particularly, because it was in his power to have restrained excursions or to have sent on a force which would justify invasion. I very much fear this unhappy affair will depopulate the county.

You will easily conceive the very unpleasant situation the inhabitants are thrown into. What will be the result, God only knows. Before I conclude, I will mention the killed and wounded. Of ours, 5 killed, 7 wounded 63 prisoners, about 18 or 20 of which were soldiers, the rest were inhabitants and they were paroled. From the best accounts we can get, the British had

> *about 60 killed and wounded. Col. Macdonald was wounded in the leg with a grape shot early in the action. I have endeavored to give a full and accurate statement, and I have no objection to your making such use of it as you may think proper.*[119]

The reactions of Ford and other locals who were against the war were predictable. They put the blame for the attack squarely on the shoulders of Captain Forsyth. As someone put it in a letter to the *New York Herald* on March 3, "His whole conduct during the winter on the St. Lawrence has been irritating in the extreme and calculated to invite retaliatory aggressions on the part of the British. He will be called to account for the distress which he has wantonly brought on our unprotected frontier." A week later, another letter appeared in the paper claiming that a committee had gone over to Prescott five days after the attack to seek compensation for damage done to private property. General Dearborn himself, commanding at Sackets Harbor, was thought to be secretly gloating over the attack of the fiercely neutral Ogdensburgh. As Louis Hasbrouck put it, "General Dearborn, it is said, expressed much satisfaction with our disaster and have no doubt felt a secret wish that our whole county might be cut off, hoping thereby to rouse the people and make the war more popular. The reverse, however, is the case."[120]

Although some considered the attack a just reaction to Forsyth's provocations, others were not as easily cowed, at least verbally. Silvius Hoard told John Ross that he met Colonel Thomas Benedict over in Rossie shortly after the attack and that Benedict told him that if he were made commander, he would invade Canada within twenty-four hours and take "ample vengeance" for his personal loss of $2,000 as a result of the ransacking.[121] Benedict, who was in search of a commission in the regular army, was actually quite fortunate from a professional point of view. He had written Parish in February asking for his intercession with the Secretary of War to secure him an appointment in the regular army.[122] However, it did not come through, and as a result of his rejection, he was able to write, "Thank God Ogdensburgh did not fall while I commanded there."

One can only imagine what a chilling effect this attack had on the inhabitants of Ogdensburg and the injury to the already depressed economic health of the area. Many families left town for safer environs, and land sales, which were already "palsied" (in Rosseel's terms), were nonexistent. Rosseel wrote to Parish that he was afraid more U.S. troops would be stationed there, and since the barracks had been destroyed, that they would be quartered in private homes.[123] David Parish let it be known to his acquaintances in the

Madison government in no uncertain terms that he believed federal troops on the St. Lawrence would do more harm than good and that the British would not attack again unless "provoked" by the presence of American troops. This astonishing position, in which a foreigner could propose to the American government that the defense of American territory could be considered a provocation to be avoided at all costs, was apparently acceded to by the Madison administration.

So, the troops never came. The British visited regularly under a flag of truce to trade at Parish's store, mostly for tea.[124] The threat of further hostilities kept prospective settlers away and destroyed what little commerce had been built up over the last few years. If it weren't for smuggling, there would have been almost no commerce of any kind. A newspaper clipping discusses the activity over in Prescott and compares it to Ogdensburg: "Our side of the river presents quite a different scene. Destitute of business, tired of inactivity, tortured by reports, sickened by illusive hopes and without the least shadow of protection, the inhabitants of this village and its vicinity are in a very unenviable situation."[125]

The situation never really improved. Ogdensburg was left to its own devices for the rest of the war. David Parish and others let it be known that they felt a military presence in Ogdensburg was actually a liability and not an advantage, and the United States never again posted troops along the river where they could have easily controlled enemy boat traffic. By chasing Forsyth out of Ogdensburg, Colonel MacDonell seems to have thwarted the only chance the Americans had to control the St. Lawrence and cut off the vital supply line from Montreal to the rest of Upper Canada. The British fort at Prescott, later named in honor of the Duke of Wellington,[126] was nearly complete by the summer of 1813, and never again during the war would the Americans contest the control of the St. Lawrence.

Colonel MacDonell spent much of the next half century trying to get the British public and government to understand how important his victory was, but without much success. He became bitter and complained that one of the reasons he was not given more recognition was that he was a Catholic.

In any event, if the British and Americans did not understand the strategic importance of the St. Lawrence River, the Canadians themselves did. Realizing how easy it would be to isolate Montreal from Upper Canada, the Canadians later constructed a series of canals to connect the Ottawa River with the St. Lawrence, far enough inland so as not to be vulnerable to any American attack. The Rideau Canal is still in operation between Ottawa and Kingston.

Chapter 5

JUST FOLLOWING ORDERS: THE CASE AGAINST LIEUTENANT LORING AUSTIN

Even today, getting from Boston to Archangel is not for the faint of heart, nor the thin of wallet. The eleven-hour flight from Logan International to Moscow is followed by a four-hour delay before the two-hour Aeroflot flight to Archangel. But this modern-day test of stamina pales in comparison to the oceangoing version that Loring Austin undertook in March 1811.

Loring was the second son of prominent Massachusetts soldier and public servant Jonathan Loring Austin and his wife, Hannah Ivers. He was born in the comfortable family home in Boston in 1790 and christened there May 1, 1790. His father was a Harvard graduate who served with the rank of major during the Revolution while living in Kittery, Maine. He was sent to Paris in 1778 to inform Dr. Benjamin Franklin of the surrender of Burgoyne, and while there, Franklin sent him on a secret mission to London to confer with members of the opposition party in British Parliament. He did not return to America until three years later and was later captured in Europe while trying to secure a loan for Massachusetts. After the war, he was a merchant in New Hampshire and held various civil offices for the Commonwealth of Massachusetts.[127]

Loring was sent on a mission by his father in the spring of 1811 to try to establish some trading contacts with the Russians through the port of Archangel, a grimy port city only two hundred miles from the Arctic Circle but whose port was open all year long due to the warmth of the Gulf Stream. Russia was fully occupied with the Napoleonic War at the time, and Archangel was the only Russian port that was open even during the dead of winter. Predictably, his mission did not go well. He was only twenty-one years old and had no experience as an international merchant, plus the fact that the Russian system of commerce was as obtuse back then as it is in the twenty-first century. He struggled to make even the smallest of trade deals and finally told his father it would never come to pass and that he was homeward bound.

Loring's mission, devoid of any accomplishments, ended in the fall of 1811 with his harrowing journey back home, which took 134 days. He wrote to his father of the terrors of being on a ship in the dead of the long subarctic night in howling gales, ships crashing into each other in the pitch-black fury of mountainous seas, the constant fear of being attacked by pirates and the humiliation of having to depend on the British navy for protection: "To our shame it must be confessed that our flag waves in the Baltic the very emblem of impotence and our commerce, persecuted by the French and the Danes, finds its only security under the British flag, a protection we cannot request without disgrace, or which perhaps may not be granted without some sarcastic remark upon our national imbecility too galling to be made with impunity but too obviously just to admit of reply."

Seven years after his voyage began, Loring was a decorated war hero but in so much financial and legal trouble that the United States Congress had to pass a special bill for his relief. How did his life become so complicated? The answer lay with Nathan Ford's nemesis: Alexander Richards, Esquire.

Not much is known about Alexander Richards's early life. He was from New London, Connecticut, and later moved to New Jersey, where he became acquainted with the Ogden family. He was hired by the Ogdens to be their land agent for the town of Madrid, and he moved there by 1803,[128] by which time he had married Sophia Tracey. He was obviously well educated and was a lawyer who was appointed to the Court of Common Pleas and was county clerk in 1811, replacing the Federalist Louis Hasbrouck, and occupied several other positions in county government. He also served in the New York State Assembly in 1808–09 and was the supervisor for the Town of Madrid. He lived in what is now called Waddington (then called Hamilton) at the corner of LaGrasse and St. Lawrence Avenue. Hamilton was the largest settlement in the town of Madrid, one of the original Ten Towns, and Madrid had the largest population of any town in the county in 1810, eclipsing even Oswegatchie.

By April 1811, Richards had somehow acquired an appointment to be the collector of the new Oswegatchie Customs District, which had been created on March 2, 1811, and split in half Collector Hart Massey's territory, which extended from the Oswego River to Massena. This meant that Richards was now the chief customs officer and import-export inspector. Nathan Ford's brother David was appointed cashier at the same time.[129] The new district may have been at least partly the result of David Parish's suggesting to the Secretary of the Treasury that Ogdensburg could become a U.S. port of entry.[130] The pay for collector was a respectable $500 per year, and his appointment was purely political in those pre–Civil Service test days. All that really mattered was party affiliation (no Federalists need apply), and Republicans were a little thin on the ground in St. Lawrence County, to put it mildly. We can almost imagine the vetting process:

"Name?"
"Alex Richards."
"Republican?"
"Yep."
"Welcome to Treasury."

Richards's district consisted of the entire northern border of St. Lawrence County, which would be nearly impossible to patrol today even with all the technology we have at hand. Richards had no technology other than a quill pen, a horse and presumably some sort of boat to serve as revenue cutter with which to enforce the federal customs duties, and he hated Embargo and Non-Intercourse Acts. Tax collectors are rarely held in high esteem by those who pay the taxes, and a collector of customs duties fared no better in that regard—and perhaps even a little worse. Although probably personally well liked, many people living on the river would undoubtedly do what they could to avoid his detection. The only real money to be made in St. Lawrence County until well into the century was made by rafting logs, grain, shingles, ashes, pelts, etc. down the river to the market in Montreal, where they could be exchanged for good, solid reliable English coin of the realm. Ever since 1809, any trade with the British in Canada was illegal, effectively cutting off the only means of economic survival for many of the residents of the county. As a strongly Federalist region, there was very little sympathy for anyone trying to enforce the ban against trading with Canada, and smuggling was considered necessary and almost a patriotic duty.

In fact, the anti-embargo sentiment was so strong that Alexander Richards was convicted of interfering with smuggling operations in January 1813 and fined by Judge Nathan Ford, no slouch himself when it came to smuggling.

The case may have been connected to a draft of one hundred militiamen overseen by Colonel John G. Fancher of the 153rd Regiment on January 15, 1813. A letter printed in the *Ogdensburgh Palladium* states that the intention of the draft was to prevent smuggling in the lower end of the county, and the writer of the letter asks if even the governor himself has the right to turn citizen-soldiers into customs-house officers. The writer also mentions that the men were threatened with the use of Forsyth's men as draft enforcers.[131]

The hatred between Nathan Ford and Alexander Richards ran deep and overpowered either man's ability to deal with the other on a rational basis. Ford's hatred of the Democrats in general was hardly a secret. When Richards ran for Assembly in 1813, David Ford said he was surprised, probably because of the political trouble Richards had been in. Nathan wrote back to his brother, "You seem surprised that the Democrats would vote for Richards. They would vote for Beelzebub to support [their] party."[132]

Three months after his return from Russia in March 1812, the United States declared war on England, and Loring Austin wanted to join the regular army, no doubt inspired by his father's career. At first, he was offered the post of cornet in the Light Dragoons but was proud of his heritage and perhaps had an overblown opinion of his own abilities. As a result, he wrote to Secretary of War Eustis declining the post, declaring that "justice to myself and friends forbids my acceptance of so inferior a situation." The Secretary apparently reconsidered and offered him a Second Lieutenancy, which he accepted in a letter written on October 12, 1812, with an effective date of September 28, 1812. He was then detailed to the large military base at Sackets Harbor.

Within a year, Alexander Richards started the whole affair that would bring Austin nothing but misery. Since Richards's battle against smuggling in general and Nathan Ford, "smuggler in chief" in particular, was not going well, he decided to see if the federal army would help him enforce these federal trade regulations. So in March 1813, not even two weeks after having lost the appointment as St. Lawrence County clerk, he wrote to General Henry Dearborn, then the commanding officer at Sackets Harbor in neighboring Jefferson County, to ask for help. However, the very week that the letter got to Sackets Harbor, General Dearborn left the place for the Niagara frontier. Upon learning this, Richards then sent a copy of his previous letter to the new interim commander at Sackets Harbor, Colonel Zebulon Pike of Pike's Peak fame:

Madrid, Mar. 16, 1813

Sir,

The practice of smuggling has become so general in this district and the plans of those engaged in it so systemized it's impossible for the Customs House officers, with all their diligence, to detect them. If a speedy stop is not put to this nefarious traffic, I fear the whole country will become disaffected to the government and engage in it. Ensign Robinson, who is now at Sackets Harbor, a vigilant and discreet officer of the volunteer militia, was formerly stationed with a guard at Massena. While there, he put a stop to smuggling in that quarter. If you thought proper to assign him to the same command, he might volunteer fifteen men here who may be depended upon, and with the aid of the Custom House officers, would put a total stop to the intercourse with Canada. The officers from Prescott are over to Ogdensburgh daily. Yesterday, one with several Indians came over in pursuit of deserters. There is no one there to molest or make them afraid.

Sir,

The above is a copy of a letter I wrote Gen. Dearborn at the date of it. Since learning he had left the command, I have thought it prudent to send a copy to you for your information. The smugglers are growing daily so bold it will be impossible to execute the laws without the aid of the military. Several of our inhabitants are going as they please within the British lines—one of the Inspectors some few days ago returning with loads he had seized near the lines met several Indians, one of whom put a paper into the hands of the smugglers who afterwards told the Officers it was owing to this forbearance alone, he was not taken to Canada. If Sir we do not have immediate assistance, the laws will be trampled under foot and the [collectors] *effected to the Government in danger of their lives—could you not send for a few days 15 or 20 horse? I would also suggest the propriety of your sending for a few of the most notorious transgressors of the laws to your place for examination, or send a discreet officer to examine them here, that those who have become liable to be punished may be forwarded to Head Quarters.*

Respectfully, Your Obt Svt
A. Richards, Collector, Oswagatchie[133]

Colonel Pike agreed that something should be done to interfere with this traitorous trade with the enemy. The following is his promise of support:

Sacketts Harbor
March 23rd 1813

Sir,

I have sent two detachments down into your quarter to punish those miscreants who possess so little patriotism as to wish success to an enemy. Any persons whom you conceive have been concerned in treasonable practices you will lodge information against in writing with a list of witnesses—and they will be apprehended—as this party will remain but a day or two with you it remains with your prudence to say how far they shall exhibit their displeasure to the disaffected.

Yours very respectfully,
Z.M. Pike
Col Comg

The two detachments Pike referred to were commanded by Lieutenant Loring Austin and Lieutenant George R. Wells of Potsdam. Austin was regular army, and Wells was detached militia. Following is a copy of the orders received by the lieutenants, orders that would have repercussions on the lives of both men for years:

Sacketts Harbor
March 25th 1813

Sir,

You are ordered to proceed to the County of St. Lawrence with your detachment. Your route will be by Watertown, Antwerp, Rossie or DeKalb and Black River. You must make enquiry of the well affected inhabitants if there are any hostile Indians or British Troops in the Country, and if there and not your superior in force, you will instantly attack them. You had best halt some distance from Ogdensburgh until you procure good intelligence. A Mr. Shaw at that place is employed to secure some public craft that is there in the ice by sinking them. When he is ready, you will draw near in order to prevent a small party crossing from Prescott and destroying the boats. This is the principal object of your march—another is for you to repair to Massena 42 Miles below Ogdensburgh and deliver the letter herewith to Mr. Richards the Collector and to seize on and make prisoners of any persons whom he charges with having been engaged in treasonable practices and bring them to this place and do any other acts which he deems will be conducive to the good of the public service. Lt. Ingram, who commands a Detachment of Riflemen, is ordered to co-operate with you and has a duplicate of this order. Being different species of Troops, it will be necessary for you to appoint places of rendezvous where you will form a junction, particularly near Ogdensburgh and Massena. When joined, the senior officer will give orders for future operations. You may hold out to the disaffected that it is not improbable but 1,000 men may be shortly established at Ogdensburgh, but to our friends assure them that until the Campaign opens, they need not expect permanent relief. Guard against spies & surprise by vigilance and frequent changes of positions. Should you make a capture of consequence, you may return as soon as you have seen the collector—if not, you may extend your excursions to the 15th April, when you will rendezvous at this place without fail. British officers of rank are frequently at Ogdensburgh. Conceal your march carefully and you may seize them. Wishing you an honorable Tour, I am

Z.M. Pike
Col Comg

The detachments began their one-hundred-mile trek from Sackets Harbor during the last week of March, and on the night of April 2–3, 1813, Lieutenant Austin, Lieutenant George R. Wells and about forty-eight dragoons and riflemen surrounded the village of Americus (Massena).[134] They got into the home of twenty-eight-year-old Uriel H. Orvis and dragged him out of bed. They did the same to Willard Seton and put both men, along with five others, in a small room with a guard ordered to kill anyone trying to escape. They reportedly verbally abused Mrs. Orvis and demanded that she feed them, which she did to the best of her ability. The next day, a similar scenario was played out, arresting more men, and again a few days later in the town of Madrid. In each case, Richards gave the lieutenants the names of men he suspected of smuggling and allowed them to apprehend his suspects. The record is not clear whether the two lieutenants stayed together acting as one body or whether each took some of the soldiers and arrested different men in different locations. In either case, by April 5, it appears that all who were going to be in custody had already been captured.

Thirteen men altogether were arrested in this manner and herded to Hamilton (now Waddington), where four were released by Richards for whatever reasons. The other nine were marched up the shore of the St. Lawrence to Ogdensburg, at which place one more man, George C. Conant, was also set free. The remaining eight men[135] were more or less dragged to Sackets Harbor by Sergeant Hayes and confined there in the military brig while Lieutenants Austin and Wells were confronted by the civil authorities (i.e. Nathan Ford) in Ogdensburg. Since those civil authorities in Ogdensburg had no troops with which to counter Lieutenants Austin and Wells, their protestations of impropriety were just that and could not be enforced. Austin and Wells then left Ogdensburg and got as far as Old DeKalb, apparently pursued by the county sheriff and perhaps some deputies.

It is not quite clear what happened in DeKalb, but it seems that Austin and Wells were surrounded and told that they were being arrested for having illegally detained the nine men. When it appeared there was no way out of their dilemma, Austin wrote to Pike from DeKalb asking for help. In part, he said, "Against my known enemies, Sir, I have always proceeded with caution, but these scoundrels have entrapped both him [Wells] and myself totally unprepared. The United States can surely afford myself and Lt. Wells the necessary bail [$12,000]. It is too large a sum to warrant any appeal to my friends. For Heaven's sake, Sir, exert authority to extricate us from these disguised enemies and oblige."[136] Just as they were to be taken into custody, Lieutenant Austin got off another note to Pike on April 10 with the following plea: "They seem here resolute to carry this question to the extremity and appear somewhat fearful that an armed force may be ordered to release me from their iniquitous confinement; not by absolute compulsion but by an urgent and repeated request, I shall accompany the Sheriff to Ogdensburg this evening, which place I presume they will make my residence till released."[137]

Both officers were confined in the jail in Ogdensburg on nine counts each of trespass, assault and false imprisonment, charges that they were scheduled to answer in the Court of Common Pleas on June 1, 1813. Bail was originally set at $12,000 each, but by April 10, Judge Nathan Ford imposed the punitive bail of $90,000 on them, a figure amounting to over $1 million in today's money. As one paper put it, "The sum is not too large if our liberties are yet esteemed any value."[138]

An early view of Ogdensburg from the site of Fort Van Rensselaer. The building on the right with the cupola is the old courthouse, in which Austin and Wells were confined. *Courtesy of the Ogdensburg Public Library.*

The crux of the matter was this: the American system of law is based on civilian officials enforcing all laws, and any person suspected of breaking a law has to be arrested by those civilian officials, under specific warrants listing specific charges. Grand juries return indictments for felonies, and civilian courts try those cases in front of duly elected or appointed judges. Colonel Pike, acting in concert with Alexander Richards, broke all those rules. Pike sent a blank warrant to be filled out by Richards with any names he so desired, without formal charges or the involvement of any legitimate court or grand jury. Then, Richards had U.S. Army personnel arrest and transport the prisoners to a military jail in another county and held them without bail or formal charges. Unless martial law had been declared, the entire sad incident was illegal and contrary to everything in American legal tradition.[139]

The eight prisoners at Sackets Harbor were held for forty-eight hours and then transferred to the custody of Amos Benedict, the Jefferson County district attorney, after he informed Pike that their detention was illegal and improper. They were freed from the jail in Watertown within ten days by a writ of habeas corpus obtained in Utica, but that did nothing to allay the outrage that many people felt upon hearing of the incident. As the *Ogdensburgh Palladium* put it, "Thus were eight American citizens, after being seized in a violent manner and dragged 130 miles from their homes, left to return as they could, at the breaking up of winter when the roads are almost impassable, without any charge having been exhibited against them, or any examination or enquiry whatever relative to their conduct."[140]

Alexander Richards should have known better, being a lawyer himself and a former judge. He knew very well that the whole affair was really his way of getting around his old enemy Nathan Ford. He also should have known that, given Ford's almost pathological hatred of him, coupled with the judge's well-known disdain for the war and anyone involved in it, that there would be hell to pay if things went wrong. And things had gone very wrong.

As so often happens in struggles between powerful men, the powerful men themselves did not get hurt, but their underlings did. Colonel Pike had nothing to fear from Nathan Ford, surrounded as he was by thousands of soldiers. Alex Richards really was not too worried about being able to survive any repercussions, as he had been fighting with Ford for years. The men arrested in Massena were certainly roughly handled but were soon freed and went on with their lives with visions of lucrative lawsuits against the men who had arrested them and abrogated their rights. The only two people who did suffer in this whole sordid affair were Austin and Wells, imprisoned for following direct orders given by their commanding officer. Austin wrote to Pike several times practically begging for help in raising bail money, but to no avail. Pike was not unsympathetic, but he had no real idea of what the next steps could or should be. Pike wrote to Secretary of War John Armstrong to apprise him of the situation, probably realizing that he had overstepped his bounds, but at least at first, there was no help coming from that quarter. As a result, the two lieutenants were stuck in jail, awaiting trial. Ford also ordered the arrest of Zebulon Pike himself but had no way to enforce it.[141]

Austin had written for help, assuming that since he was acting under direct orders, he would be freed in a matter of days. However, Pike was busy with other matters, mainly planning an attack on York, the capital of Upper Canada. He realized that his military interference into the laws of New York State had caused this uproar and that further incursions by him into that forbidden territory were unlikely to help.

When the story broke in April 1813, many newspapers, particularly the Federalist ones, linked Pike's actions to the Madison administration and implied that Loring Austin's mission was a plot to deprive citizens of their constitutional rights. Some papers, however, put the Massena incident in a different light altogether and portrayed it as a defense of the nation against the British, who were conspiring with smugglers to obtain intelligence. The *Albany Argus* wrote, "As Great Britain has a deep interest in having our laws violated and in obtaining information through smugglers, she and her friends will no doubt attempt to raise the hue and cry: but every patriot will rejoice at the detection of a practice fraught with dire evils to our country."[142]

The most widely read account of the affair appeared first in the *Utica Patriot* on April 13, 1813, and its headline left little to the imagination: "Rights of the Citizens of the State of New York Trampled Underfoot and the CONSTITUTION Violated by the Military Officers of the United States." The story that followed ignited a firestorm of criticism and was passed around to all sympathetic newspapers. Pike himself saw the article and immediately understood the ramifications of his orders to Austin and Wells.[143] The Federalist paper *Northern Whig* published as cogent and concise a summation of the issue as any other paper and tied the solution to the problem to the elections to be held the next week:

> *Military Despotism: It is the practice of the leading Democrats, when you point out to them the high-handed measures of government and the tendency which they have to destroy the country, to turn from you with a sneer, insisting upon it that the liberties of the country are not endangered. Let the reader turn to that part of this paper, where under the above head*[line] *are detailed some transactions not to be sneered at and which speak for themselves as to the manner in which the liberties of the citizen are trampled upon by the government and its officers. In scarcely any other country in this world, except in France, could a military officer with impunity have thus sat at defiance the civil law of the country by rearing its inhabitants from their homes under an escort of soldiery. In England, as debased and polluted as the government of that country is said to be, the officer who should have dared to perpetrate such an outrage upon the liberties of its citizens would have forfeited his life. In this country, however, we shall be told that it is all an innocent and harmless piece of business. But the reader needs to not be told that these "innocent harmless pieces of business" are multiplying upon the country, and if not immediately corrected by the voices of the people through the ballot boxes, they will, when the evil has grown to such a height as to render it impracticable to resort to this mode of redress, be compelled to submit to it or to resist it in the field at the expense of their blood and at the risk of their lives.*[144]

At that time, Austin and Wells were still in the jail in the rear of the courthouse on Euphemia Street in Ogdensburg, and Colonel Pike knew he needed to extricate himself from the developing public relations nightmare. As he wrote on April 14, "Lt. Austin was ordered to assist the Collector in the enforcement of civil authority, and not in its violation, at least that was my intention. If he has exceeded his orders, he has done wrong; if they were too extensive, it was due to a want of legal knowledge. But I hope you will suggest some mode by which these young men can be liberated from this unpleasant situation which they submitted to out of respect for Civil Authority."[145] The Federalists made sure to fan the flames of indignation and took advantage of every opportunity to flay the Democrats with the rhetoric of "military despotism." Nathan Ford wrote of the incident to David Parish in Philadelphia, and Parish replied that he had dined with Secretary of the Treasury Gallatin and apprised him of the role his customs collector played in the affair.[146]

Although Ford was the main cheerleader in this rally against military despotism, his was not the only voice heard in the crowd. Louis Hasbrouck, who was a fairly mild-mannered lawyer and civic-minded citizen, wrote, "They may as well proclaim martial law at once and do away all the civil rights. No man is safe that does not do homage to the noble Colonel [Pike] and his worthy coadjutor, [Alexander] Richards."[147]

Pike would not be able to help for very long. He sailed from Sackets Harbor with the rest of the army stationed there on April 25, heading for Little York (now Toronto), the provincial capital of Upper Canada on the north shore of Lake Ontario. The American force captured the town on April 27, burned the Parliament building and routed the defenders. Just as the British were evacuating the garrison, they touched off the powder magazine to keep it from falling into the hands of the Americans. The resulting cataclysmic explosion hurled rocks, bricks and other debris hundreds of yards and killed several men, including thirty-four-year-old Zebulon Pike himself, whose body was returned to Sackets Harbor for burial.

The despair felt by Austin and Wells upon hearing of Pike's death can only be imagined. He held the key to their salvation, as it was on his orders that they came to St. Lawrence County in the first place. Who would protect them now? They were lowly lieutenants stuck in an out-of-the-way jail, held to astronomical bail, while the rest of the U.S. Army was hundreds of miles away fighting the next campaign. The situation must have seemed hopeless. And newspapers, if they were allowed access to any, would have been of the Federalist camp, so they would be reading about their own demonization and calls for retribution. Their mood could not have been lightened by their realization that justice, at least in this case, was not blind. They soon understood that by having Judge Nathan Ford hold the keys not only to their jail cells but also to their futures in general, they were in for real trouble. Ford was without a doubt the most vindictive and prejudiced adversary they could have faced, as he took a personal, political and professional delight in prosecuting the two officers. This was based partly on his genuine philosophical convictions as an American and Federalist and his outrage at this egregious violation of the Constitution, but there is no denying that he used the two lieutenants as proxies against the Democratic Party in general and Alexander Richards in particular. The case suited Ford's sense of self-righteousness and allowed him to be the bully while masquerading as the protector of the people, blurring the line between prosecution and persecution. Letter after letter to his brother during this time reveal his seething hatred for Richards and anyone connected with him and the Democratic Party. He wrote at least one article for the *Palladium* ridiculing Richards and introducing his meanest slurs against him by referring to him as "the Pope" and as "Prefect," terms that he often repeated.

The bail records of that time no longer exist, so it is not possible to say exactly when Austin and Wells were freed from jail, but it was apparently some time in the early summer.[148] Ford wrote to his brother on May 16 that General Brown was working on getting them out of jail, with $9,000 bail each. They and Alexander Richards were being sued by all nine men: the eight who were sent to Sackets Harbor, as well as George C. Conant, who was released at Ogdensburg. Although originally scheduled to answer the charges at the June 1, 1813 Court of Common Pleas, the cases may have been transferred to the Circuit Court of Oyer and Terminer, scheduled to meet on June 16. However, that session was mysteriously and abruptly cancelled. The political climate in St. Lawrence County was so poisoned in the summer of 1813 that any and every variation from the norm was seen as an attempt by one side or the other to subvert the judicial process in the heavily Federalist county. Rumors were rife as to the cause of such an unusual occurrence. There were many high-profile cases to be argued, and suspicions were immediately aroused. Benjamin Raymond of Potsdam wrote to Chief Justice James Kent, brother of Jefferson County's Moss Kent, to get to the bottom of the cause:

Potsdam, June 25, 1813

Sir,

Much surprise has been produced in this county by the omission to hold the Circuit Court of Oyer and Terminer of this week. Grand and Petit jurors were summoned, witnesses subpoenaed, and from the remote parts of the county were on their way to court when information was received that the Judge had concluded not to convene. Very serious injury might be sustained by many persons in consequence of the measure, as more business was ready than at any former circuit, and some of it of a very interesting nature. Some criminals are in confinement without indictment, and some other presentments are to be made.

The surprise existing is in no way allayed by the contradictory reports as to the cause of the omission. It is ascertained that the first information that no court would be held came from Judge [Alexander] *Richards and that he had sent an express to Judge* [Joseph C.] *Yates to ascertain the fact. As he is plaintiff in a number of slander suits in which the defendants are all anxious and ready for trial, the suspicion is pretty general that Judge Y[ates], ignorant of the particular interest of Judge R*[ichards], *has been induced from some information received from the latter of the danger of coming to this county etc. to the step he has taken.*

Will you sir, (if proper) inform me of the real reason that the court was not held and at what time we might probably expect it to be held?[149]

Nathan Ford was also somewhat taken aback that the court had been cancelled, but he revealed that Raymond may himself have had more than a passing interest in the delay. In a letter to his brother, he wrote, "We have no circuit. Judge Yates is fearful that his valuable carcass would be sought after. This he need not have feared. The whole business of the County is to go over for a year. This prevents the judgments against Raymond in favor of J. Phoenix and also Muir."[150]

A letter apparently written by Nathan Ford on May 4, 1813, appeared in the *New York Herald* in which he complains about the U.S. Mail being interdicted and no newspapers allowed to be delivered to Ogdensburg. He also gloats about the fact that the men arrested by Austin and Wells were now free and that the officers themselves had been arrested, saying that the whole affair was an "unheard-of attempt to execute military law upon our citizens and that 'Pope' [Richards] was to fill the office of denouncer." He added the warning that "the people of St. Lawrence will not suffer their rights to be trampled upon." It is a case of delicious irony that Nathan Ford himself, just fifteen years earlier, while acting as a Herkimer County magistrate, said that he would love to be able to act against the men who had been stealing his hemlock bark if Herkimer County would just send him the "processes" and he would fill in the names later.[151]

In any event, by November 1813, Austin was serving as General Jacob Brown's aide-de-camp,[152] having been promoted to first lieutenant on September 3, 1813. At the behest of no less a patron than General Jacob Brown himself, Lieutenant Austin was offered a captaincy in the Forty-sixth U.S. Infantry in June 1814, which allowed him to stay in Brown's corps. His commission was signed by the secretary of war and President Madison himself. He was promoted to major for his conspicuous bravery at the Battle of Chippewa on July 6, 1814. Loring Austin was a fairly good artist and drew several battle scenes and maps that survive today, his maps of French Mills being particularly interesting.

Austin spent much of the rest of the war as General Jacob Brown's aide-de-camp, and it is tantalizing to think that perhaps he got that post because Brown *did* bail him out and considered him a rising star. In any event, the War of 1812 officially ended in early 1815, and Loring wanted to continue on in the peacetime army, which was being drastically reduced. His brother James (and we assume others) wrote to the secretary of war on his behalf, and as a result, he was made a captain in the Eighth U.S. Infantry in June 1815 while again stationed at Sackets Harbor. He was soon promoted again, and Major Austin was assigned to be the head of the U.S. Army recruiting corps.

Rising star and regular army or not, Austin and Wells had been sued by the nine men taken to Ogdensburg, and the New York State Supreme Court of Judicature awarded the men damages against Austin to the tune of $6673.90 and $5716.83 against George R. Wells. The two former lieutenants also racked up legal fees over the course of the several trials and were unable even to pay those. With those judgments hanging over their heads, Austin and Wells were running out of options by mid-1817 and were fearful of losing everything they owned or might inherit. They had been ordered to pay the victims of the roundup an exorbitant sum that they could never hope to raise. They brought their legal and financial plight to the attention of Congress, and like all other claims against the government, their case was assigned to the Committee on Claims in the U.S. House of Representatives. In January 1818, the committee began considering their petition. Although in general it was disposed to vote for financial relief, the committee wanted to make sure that the two officers really were under obligation to follow the order they were given. Lieutenants Austin and Wells did not know or care about the legality or impropriety of the order itself and had never even considered not obeying. It was clear in hindsight that the involvement of federal troops in rounding up suspected smugglers was unconstitutional. But the fact is that Austin and Wells were simply following orders.

The Committee on Claims seems to have had no members with military expertise and so wrote to the secretary of war to ask his opinion of the matter. Secretary of War John C. Calhoun replied to them that whether Pike's order was legal or not, "I would respectfully suggest that there may be cases in the exigency of war in which, if the commander should transcend his legal power, Congress ought to protect him, and those who act under him, from consequential damages."[153]

The committee was still not entirely convinced. If the infraction had been merely to seize a man's property because of an illegal order, that was one thing, but to seize the man himself was something else entirely. The committee wished "to assert also the principle of the sovereignty of the civil over the military power" and so asked the United States Attorney General to rule on whether Pike's order was lawful or not, and the answer was a firm negative. Based on these two opinions, the committee forwarded its recommendation to the House that the damages be paid for the men, but only because the lieutenants were obliged to obey the order, not because the order itself was justified in any way. Therefore, it was decided that the federal government had a moral obligation to protect the two former lieutenants from the certain financial ruin that would come from the civil judgments against them.[154]

As a result, on April 20, 1818, the U.S. House of Representatives passed a bill entitled "An Act for the Relief of Major Loring Austin and George R. Wells." The bill called for the U.S. Treasury to pay Austin's $6673.90 plus $607.26 in legal fees. It also called for the payment of George R. Wells's judgment of $5716.83, plus $687.04.

Freed from the burden of an unpayable debt, Loring Austin married his sweetheart, Sarah Wendell Orne, on October 24, 1818. He died on January 31, 1826.

Chapter 6

WILKINSON'S FLOATING CIRCUS

For the most part, the United States has been blessed in times of national distress with leaders, both military and political, who rose to the occasion and ensured the ultimate victory of the country. The saga of General James Wilkinson stands out as perhaps the single most conspicuous exception to that trend. When the United States needed a vibrant, bold leader, it got Wilkinson's vacillating weakness instead. When the United States needed a true patriot and loyal citizen, it got the traitorous double agent Wilkinson instead. And when the United States needed a strong, heroic leader, the infirm, vacillating and possibly drug-addicted Wilkinson again showed up. Of all the fakers, frauds and fools who have trotted across the stage of American history, James Wilkinson stands out as a scoundrel among scoundrels, almost entirely devoid of character yet somehow placed in critical positions of command time after time.

Wilkinson embodied most of the major failings of the senior officer corps American army during the War of 1812, being a washed-up re-tread from the Revolutionary War of nearly thirty years earlier. His outdated experience and mediocre leadership may not have been fatal flaws if he had had at least some redeeming qualities as a human being, and of these, he seems to have been almost completely deficient. His most glaring shortcoming, and the one for which he gained his infamy, was his willingness to trade his patriotism for personal gain. He was famously described as having "never won a battle or lost a court-martial."

General James Wilkinson.

The United States more or less abandoned the St. Lawrence frontier after the capture of Ogdensburg in February 1813, and instead of fortifying the border and choking off the resupply of British forces in the Great Lakes, the Madison administration decided to fight the British at the far western edges of the conflict. The folly of this policy was not lost on Nathan Ford, who almost certainly was the author of a note printed in the *Ogdensburgh Palladium* of May 19, 1813,[155] in which a comment on the constant fortification of Prescott was followed by this observation: "What a pity our great men at the head of the nation do not devote more time to the study of geography of this frontier, instead of contriving plans to keep themselves in office and ensure the election of their state tools."

The British were hardly idle on the St. Lawrence in the spring of 1813. They took advantage of the lack of American presence on the river to increase their fortification of Prescott, shifting more troops to be stationed there and constantly adding to and refining their defenses. All of this military activity was easily observable from Ogdensburg, and with a flair for irony he was not normally known for, Louis Hasbrouck wrote, "They have pitched about 100 of our tents which we lent them last winter."[156]

William Gilkison of Prescott, who was a leading citizen, merchant captain and spy, was busy going back and forth to Ogdensburg making sure no military measures were being taken in secret.[157] He need not have worried.

In the spring of 1813, General James Wilkinson was ordered to leave his post in Louisiana and head north to take over operations in the Lake Ontario-St. Lawrence River theater. He had recently been promoted to major general but exhibited one of his many character defects when it took him almost four months to complete the journey, finally showing up in Sackets Harbor on August 20, 1813. His mission was to "reduce" Kingston either directly or indirectly, as he saw fit, and thereby cut the British supply line that ran up the St. Lawrence River. The overall plan was to combine General John Boyd's forces at Fort George with those under Generals Swartout and Brown at Sackets Harbor, creating an invasion force of about seven thousand men that would then campaign down the St. Lawrence.[158]

Shortly after arriving at Sackets Harbor, Wilkinson headed to Fort George on the Niagara River to confer with General Boyd but ended up spending a month there sick in bed. By the end of September 1813, he was planning to get back to Sackets, bringing with him some of General Boyd's force that had been bottled up at Fort George all summer. He was reluctant to return to the harbor because John Armstrong, the Secretary of War, was there, and it would be difficult for him to shirk his duty while under the watchful eye of his superior.

By the end of September, the requisite number of watercraft had been assembled at Fort George, and General Boyd's army began its move down the lake to Henderson Harbor, a few miles south of Sackets Harbor. Fort George was left in the capable hands of Colonel Winfield Scott and his Second Artillery Regiment. Wilkinson himself left Fort George and arrived back at Sackets on October 4, while Boyd's army arrived at Henderson Harbor in dribs and drabs over the course of the next few days, not completely in place until October 15. Boyd's tardiness did not actually set the operation back, since Wilkinson was once again sick in bed until the middle of the month.

In theory, everything was in readiness for the assault on Kingston once Wilkinson recovered and Boyd's men were in place. General Jacob Brown had been very busy in Wilkinson's absence, assembling boats, boatmen, horses and the various supplies an army of seven thousand men might need on an extended mission.

The late autumn weather in that part of the world is quite unpredictable. Warm, sunny days are almost as likely as snow squalls, and of course there was no such thing as a weather forecast at the time. Still, with the number of lives at stake, commencing a risky plan at that time of year was foolhardy in the extreme. However, the constant delays and high expectations from Washington precluded the vain Wilkinson from admitting that his plan was not feasible. If he could have found a plausible scapegoat, he almost certainly would have cancelled the mission altogether, for here it was eight weeks after his arrival at Sackets Harbor, and nothing of military importance had yet been accomplished.

While waiting at Sackets Harbor for Boyd's men to complete their trip and for the weather to clear, Wilkinson sent a contingent of mounted troops down the shore of the St. Lawrence. On October 13, 1813, seventy men of Lieutenant Colonel Nelson Luckett's regiment of U.S. First Dragoons entered Ogdensburg from the Morristown road, ostensibly on a reconnaissance mission. They encamped in the vacant lot behind Russell's tavern in Ogdensburg until Captain Henry Jackson of the Royal Artillery across the river in Prescott saw them in his telescope and began firing his two twenty-four-pound cannons, located at the southeast and southwest corners of the new fort. The first shots fell harmlessly in the village, and although Luckett was flattered by the attention, he did not want to get flattened by it and so was convinced to move his forces out of Ogdensburg into the backcountry near Heuvelton, which he did with admirable alacrity. However, while they were still saddling up, one shell passed over their heads and through the upstairs county courtroom, a 7,200-foot shot from Fort Wellington, lodging in a partition wall just minutes after the grand jury had been evacuated by Judge Benjamin Raymond.[159]

Suspicions were aroused in Ogdensburg that perhaps Colonel Luckett's visit was not strictly for military reconnaissance, especially when he returned the next morning, paraded very visibly near the shore, and was greeted with the same solid-shot salutation from Prescott. After all, what would General Wilkinson NOT already know about the American side of the river? As John Ross wrote to David Parish, perhaps Alexander Richards was somehow involved, his intention being to interfere with the court: "The clandestine object of their infamous manouevers [*sic*] was to break up the court, which however had not and will not succeed in spite of the Pope [Richards] and all his gang, who will soon feel the force of law."[160]

By October 16, 1813, Lieutenant Colonel Luckett had dispersed his men along the shore of the St. Lawrence downstream from Ogdensburg to act as pickets, presumably to prevent spies from either side crossing. At 10:00 p.m. that night, Major Francis Cockburn, commanding the Canadian Fencibles at Prescott, crossed the river and attacked and captured a Dragoon lieutenant

The original St. Lawrence County courthouse in Ogdensburg.

and seven privates who were stationed at Scott's tavern at Red Mills in the town of Lisbon. He also captured nine of their horses and tack, which were auctioned off in Canada, with the proceeds divided among the captors.[161] During the skirmish, a sergeant and a private were killed as they fired from inside the tavern in which they were stationed. Another private was gravely wounded. Luckett hereafter decided that the home of Peter Wells on the road to Canton might be a safer place to bivouac[162] while he and his troops laid low, waiting to join up with Wilkinson when he eventually made his way down the river.

The many delays suffered by the Americans in September and October allowed the British to beef up their defenses at Kingston, causing the Secretary of War to change his mind and more or less order Wilkinson to bypass Kingston and head directly for Montreal. Wilkinson was hesitant to leave such a large garrison in his rear as he headed down the St. Lawrence, and Commodore Chauncey, who was supposed to play a large part in the attack on Kingston, now chafed at being reassigned to a much less important role as mere guardian of the rear echelon.

Wilkinson himself finally left Sackets Harbor on October 17, 1813, and headed for Grenadier Island, about halfway between Sackets Harbor and the head of the St. Lawrence. Grenadier Island made an ideal staging area because of its location and good harbor. When Wilkinson's force landed at Grenadier Island in October 1813, he had about 7,300 men, twenty-two pieces of field artillery and seventeen siege pieces, which he would need to capture Montreal. This would be the largest American military force assembled until the Civil War almost fifty years later. However, it took days to transfer all the men and supplies to the island, and several boats, including some with much-needed rations and equipment, were lost in the high waves or dashed up on rocky shoals as they were trying to get to the island.

Wilkinson saw that the loss of food and supplies was severe, but he had no alternatives. Because squalls and heavy winds had scattered many of the troop transports, it was another week before all the units were reformed and ready to sail again. Just as Wilkinson was about to begin his mission, heavy snow followed by a stinging, wind-driven rain pelted his force for days. The raw weather did nothing to improve the fragile health of the aging Wilkinson, and he was again under the care of a doctor.

As he waited on Grenadier Island for the weather to clear, Wilkinson sent Colonel Joseph G. Swift, his chief engineer, and some of his assistants to scout the waters of the St. Lawrence near Prescott, since the flotilla would somehow have to pass that heavily fortified place. Swift and his men arrived in Ogdensburg on October 23 and began their reconnoitering. Canadian captain Reuben Sherwood of the Glengarry Fencibles was informed that high-ranking officers were in the area and proceeded to make their lives miserable, forcing them to do most of their scouting at dawn and dusk and most of their movement after dark.[163] They stayed in the area long enough to take some depth soundings and obtain a plan of the fort at Prescott.[164] John Ross mentions their activities in a letter to David Parish, which he thought prudent to write in German to protect from prying eyes.[165]

On October 29, the advanced guard under General Jacob Brown finally left Grenadier Island and sailed around Cape Vincent into the St. Lawrence, headed for the first place of rendezvous, French Creek (now Clayton), and arrived there just about dark on October 30. Other units soon followed, but it was not an easy voyage. The upper part of the river is known as the Thousand Islands, and navigating around these islands, some many acres and some no more than rocky points sticking up out of the water, was filled with danger. It was common for boats to follow the wrong channel and get separated from the others. On November 1 and 2, Brown's troops were attacked at French Creek by four British boats that had eluded the blockade set up by Commodore Chauncey.[166] However, hot shot fired by the Americans soon convinced them of the error of their ways, setting fire to the brig *Earl of Moira*, and they withdrew.

The majority of the rest of the force left Grenadier Island the first two days of November, with Wilkinson himself embarking for French Creek on November 3. The weather was awful, and the ragtag flotilla must have been a sight to see, with boats of every description chock full of men and supplies heading downriver carried mostly by the current and the steady west wind. One thing became abundantly clear: this was not going to be a surprise attack. Once clear of the Thousand Islands, the more than three hundred watercraft making up the flotilla could be seen for miles from the Canadian shore. The only thing the British were not yet sure of was the focus of the attack—would it be Prescott first or Montreal?

It is approximately 170 miles from Kingston to Montreal, and the St. Lawrence River has three distinct regions as it heads downhill toward the ocean. The uppermost part is very wide and flat, but ships are constrained by the 1,800 small islands and shoals that make up the Thousand Islands. Once past the islands, much of the next section of the St. Lawrence is also quite flat, with almost no discernable current, and sailing is easy, if not fast. But to get to Montreal, the water has to fall a distance of two hundred vertical feet from Cape Vincent, which it does mostly in a series of five rapids, and once past Ogdensburg, the sailing becomes more difficult. The Galop Rapids, just past Ogdensburg and Prescott, drop seven feet; Rapide du Plat drops about eleven feet near Waddington; Long Sault near Massena falls almost ninety feet over a distance of several miles; and then Cedars Rapids and the turbulent Lachine Rapids fall right above Montreal itself. So, the beginning part of the trip was uneventful as far as whitewater was concerned, but there was certainly the promise of excitement ahead when that many boats, guided by inexperienced crews, try to navigate some very treacherous waters.

The Royal Navy's Captain William Mulcaster and eight of his ships had eluded Commodore Chauncey, slipped out of Kingston harbor and followed the Americans to French Creek. They attacked them there on the night of November 3 and again the following morning, inflicting some casualties but not able to destroy the boats of the Americans because they had been pulled up onto the shore of French Creek.

While at French Creek on November 4, Wilkinson sent a message to Commodore Chauncey asking him to detach one of his armed schooners, such as the *Pert* (formerly David Parish's *Collector*), to provide him with extra firepower as protection against the British fleet. Chauncey, who was anchored upstream near Kingston, replied that he had the British flotilla under observation and would handle them from there, so Wilkinson had no need to worry.[167] It was a promise that Chauncey could not back up, much to Wilkinson's disadvantage. Most of November 4 was spent preparing for the next phase of the trip down the river and organizing the ships by brigade.

On Friday, November 5, the flotilla left French Creek about mid-morning. Wilkinson's idea of organizing the flotilla by brigade was an artifact of military movements on land in which a commander would ordinarily designate the order of march so as to best carry out the mission at hand. However, organizing a fleet of more than three hundred boats was not nearly as easy and would have been difficult to do on any body of water. Attempting aquatic choreography in the Thousand Islands was doomed to failure from the start because the laws of physics demand that fluids move faster through confined spaces such as the dozens of channels between the islands. Therefore, boats that were influenced by the current and wind were traveling at different speeds depending on their specific path through the myriad of channels. The islands also blocked the view of the other boats, so all was in confusion within a mile or so of leaving French Creek. The vanguard of the fleet made it all the way to Samuel Hoag's place below Morristown by sunset, but the boats were strung out all over the shore, a distance of four miles. Wilkinson wanted to run from Hoag's to the head of the Galop Rapids that night, bypassing the fort at Prescott under cover of darkness. But the plan was too raw and too dangerous, so the idea was abandoned, and the fleet stayed moored in safety overnight.[168]

Wilkinson and his brigade commanders undoubtedly went round and round at Hoag's on the night of the fifth, trying to determine the best way to get by Prescott. The harassing British boats following them, the cumulative toll on the men being cooped up in boats for days, the fact that the full moon advertized their presence, their now dwindling rations and the knowledge of rough water ahead would have all weighed heavily on their minds. The plan they came up with was probably the best one available under the circumstances.

So, they left Hoag's late in the day on Saturday, November 6, and by sundown, the flotilla had got as far as Griffin's, three miles above Ogdensburg. There they unloaded all the men and munitions and sent them overland,

"Passing Prescott" sketch by Peter Rindlisbacher. *Courtesy of Peter Rindlisbacher.*

passing in front of Nathan Ford's mansion, crossing the Oswegatchie and marching around behind Ogdensburg. A letter printed in the Herkimer *American* mentioned that as the infantry marched by Ogdensburg, the men were in such bad shape that they "resembled a moving hospital much more than they did an invading army."

The plan was to float the now-empty watercraft past the fort, manned with just enough crew to row and steer them, and then to regain the shore a mile or so beyond Prescott, safe from the enemy's cannonade. Providence seemed to be smiling on them, as that night's full moon was blanketed with a heavy fog, and the three hundred or so boats were on the move by 8:00 p.m.[169] But as luck would have it, the fog lifted part way through the operation, revealing the flotilla and seven thousand bayonets gleaming in the moonlight, and the British fort opened fire.

It appears that even though the big cannons had been deployed at Prescott for six months or more, the artillerymen attached to them had never conducted "ranging," in which shots were fired at various elevations to determine where they would land. As such, their shots, even with the moonlight reflecting off the water, did not fall where they wanted them to, and there were almost no casualties or boats lost during the float-by. However, there was some damage in the village of Ogdensburg from errant bombs and shells. One man was killed, and at least one boat went aground, with its cargo being unloaded and stored for later retrieval in Ogdensburg. But otherwise, the operation succeeded as planned, and the troops rejoined the flotilla five miles below Ogdensburg at Red Mills in Lisbon.

Wilkinson was still "indisposed," so he stayed aboard his boat and safely made it downstream to Daniel Thorp's place, about a mile below Ogdensburg, where he disembarked. Several references list the farm as Sharp's place, but Daniel Thorp himself testified that it was at his home. He was testifying about Wilkinson being at his home and what he did (or didn't do) while he was there. As mentioned before, Wilkinson was not in particularly good health during the trip down the St. Lawrence and may have been legitimately under the care of a doctor who may have prescribed laudanum or some other drug to ease his symptoms. In any case, under the influence or not, Wilkinson apparently became "jovial" shall we say and spoke his mind on many subjects, including his opinion of Nathan Ford and the residents of St. Lawrence County in general. The drug may also have exposed his musical side, as his subordinates were treated to several ditties, sung without accompaniment.

Word of this escapade soon spread to Ogdensburg, and Judge Ford let the world know just what he thought of Wilkinson, drunk or sober. The following letter, presumably originally printed in the *Ogdensburgh Palladium*, [170] appeared in the *New York Herald* and other Federalist newspapers, and Ford would feel the repercussions of this letter for months:

> *Mr. Editor*
> *Sir,*
>
> *The ungentlemanly attack made upon my character by Gen. Wilkinson has been such as to require notice from me. Will you have the goodness to publish the enclosed, and much oblige.*
>
> *Your friend,*
> *NATHAN FORD*
>
> *Ogdensburgh 10th November 1813*
>
> *TO GENERAL JAMES WILKINSON*
> *COMMANDER IN CHIEF OF THE ARMY OF THE UNITED STATES*

Sir,

In your passage down the St. Lawrence upon your expedition to Montreal, you landed your troops three miles above this village. Your illiberal and ungentlemanly abuse of my character on that day and the succeeding evening was such that none but a man of your cast would have indulged in. To prevent any mistake, I have ascertained beyond the possibility of a doubt, "You declared it to be your wish that Ogdensburgh might be burnt, and as for Judge Ford, you would hang him, and if the enemy did not burn his property, you would be God damned if you would not"—contemptible wretch! That you are much better qualified for an incendiary and a hangman than you are for a General has never been a question with me. If public opinion is a proper tribunal, you must be dull of apprehension if you have not discovered that a halter is a necessary requisite to your last elevation.

It never fails to be the case when a wretch like you accidentally gets himself laced in the situation you are, to ape the tyrant and trifle with private property and private character. Had you been separated from your army, your dastard soul would sooner have shrunk back to its primitive nothingness than you would have dared to have taken the liberty you did with my character. Your low ribaldry was so disgusting that even your political friends were ashamed, and they did that for you which you were never known to do for yourself—they blushed. When you arrived at Mr. Thorp's, which is but 4 miles from where you sat out (the night you moved the army through this village) you discovered (or others discovered it for you) that it was necessary to stop and take a nap and give time for the fumes of hot rum to evaporate. A great General requires great stimulants. There are none who will doubt your great qualities or the clearness of your head when it is known that it requires two drinks of hot rum to enable you to go through the operation of one shaving. I shall pass over your contemptible foppery at Mr. Thorp's in the display of your wife's picture and your two watches.

Your folly and your foppish behavior and conversation would have disgraced a schoolboy. After you had sufficiently gratified your vanity with these toys, you commenced your virulent abuse of me in language which would have disgraced a billingsgate. After having exhausted a full portion of your ill nature, you proposed moving on after your army. But as you had not quite filled the measure of your folly, you proposed to entertain the company with a song before you set out. For the sake of its sublimity and your taste, I will repeat one of the verses of your song:

"I am now a-going to Canada;
And there I will get money
And there I'll kiss the pretty squaws;
They are as sweet as honey."

It is no secret that money is your god, and the end has always justified the means for your obtaining it.

As for your honey squaws, that is a matter of your own; I have no doubt you prefer black to white. The generality of people in this part of the country had an idea that you were a man, somewhat above mediocrity both as a general and a gentleman. It is only necessary for you to pass through the country with an army and you leave a universal impression that you are neither. They however admit that you support with dignity your old order, Knight of the Golden Spurs.[171]

I cannot close this note without reminding you of your audacious declaration at Sackets Harbor "that you should venture to take the civil law into your own hands and apply to the President for your justification." I should inform you that you have arrived in a state that has (thank God) a judiciary who not only have the power but the spirit to punish a daring outrage, even in the character of the little sub tyrant Wilkinson. Your base conduct at New Orleans was covered over with the Presidential mantle, but I doubt whether he would dare a second time to screen you from that punishment which the insulted majority of the laws demand. I shall now leave you to the enjoyment of your billingsgate, relishing your hot rum and your honey sweet squaws.

—Nathan Ford[172]

While waiting for the fallout of his letter, Ford, along with many others, was highly critical of a so-called military plan that was so obviously doomed to failure. "My prophecy is fast becoming verified," he wrote to his brother David, who was sitting out the war in New Jersey. "I was convinced that [the] army would never get to Montreal otherwise than as prisoners of war, and in that way they might find winter quarters there."[173]

Wilkinson spent Sunday, November 7, reorganizing his flotilla and sending some men back to Ogdensburg to try and recover as much of the jettisoned equipment as they could while the British took pot shots at them all morning. They then resumed their trip down the river toward Montreal, clearing the Galop Rapids just beyond Red Mills without incident. They camped that night at Tucker Brook (Ford refers to it as Tuttles Bay in a November 13 letter to his brother), six miles below Red Mills and just upstream from Iroquois Point, at that time near the Lisbon-Madrid border. About two thousand men crossed the river there to clear the opposite bank in preparation for the crossing of the main body the next day.

After Wilkinson bypassed Prescott on his way downriver to Montreal, Lieutenant Colonel Pearson, the commander there, was quite happy to see Lieutenant Colonel Joseph Wanton Morrison and his "Corps of Observation" arrive from Kingston by boat on the evening of November 8 with a force of about 850 men carried in sixty or so bateaux. They consisted of the remnants of the Forty-ninth infantry, the second battalion of the Eighty-ninth Infantry, three companies of voltigeurs and a squadron of gunboats. This was not a big enough force to challenge Wilkinson in direct battle, but it was more than enough to harass his rear guard all the way downriver, which was precisely what Morrison intended to do. He was also accompanied by two of Admiral Yeo's small schooners, the *Beresford* and the *Sir Sidney Smith*, plus seven gunboats, all controlled by Commander William Mulcaster of the Royal Navy. The two larger boats could go no farther downstream than Prescott because of the rapids, so their men were transferred to the shallow-draft batteaux. Lieutenant Colonel Pearson offered to come along, bringing with him several companies of militia and regulars, raising Morrison's total force to about 1,200 men.

Although the main body of American troops and the British following them had passed Ogdensburg, a British detail crossed the river to Ogdensburg on the morning of the ninth, demanding the surrender of any public property that had been left there by Wilkinson's force when two of his boats ran aground and had to unload their cargo in the village. There were no American military personnel there at the time, so Judge Raymond apparently dealt with the intruders. Although Wilkinson's men had come back to get what supplies and equipment they could on the seventh, they did not have enough cargo space or time to retrieve everything. The following list shows the remaining armaments turned over to the British:

Iron 24 lb gun 9 ft 10½ inches long 4800 lbs
Iron 8 inch mortar 16 inches long 810 lbs
Brass 10 inch mortar 1 ft 9½ inches long 620 lbs
30 French muskets, repairable
25 French bayonets
4 pouches[174]

On the morning of Monday, November 8, Wilkinson's expedition floated from Tucker Brook three miles downstream to "the narrows" at White House Bay and laid over there while the Canadian bank was cleared of snipers. Matthew Gray operated a ferry there at White House,[175] so the horses of Lieutenant Colonel Nelson Luckett's First Dragoons and Major Woodford's Second Dragoons were loaded onto the largest of the boats and taken across to the Canadian side, which General Macomb had secured. The day was occupied mainly in transporting the Dragoons across the river. The Canadian militia had built an artillery strongpoint named Fort Matilda directly across from the ferry, and General Browns forces burned it to the ground.

Wilkinson took the opportunity to hold a council of war at White House to decide the next step and see if his underlings felt that victory was possible. It was quite obvious that he did not think much of their chances for success, but the council provided him a way, in his mind, to spread the blame around if things did not go well.

Wilkinson wrote down a few facts, such as that he had about seven thousand troops under his command and that they had ten days' ration of bread and twenty days' ration of meat. He also enumerated what a spy had told him about the defenses between his position and Montreal and the fact that a British force of some size had arrived at Prescott and was not very far behind them.

The formal question he posed to his generals was this: "Should the army proceed with all possible rapidity to the attack of the said city of Montreal?" Four generals signed in the affirmative: Morgan Lewis, John Boyd, Jacob Brown and Robert Swartout. However, Generals Leonard Covington and Moses Porter signed saying that the attack should continue because there was no other alternative—hardly a ringing vote of confidence. It was thus decided to continue on to Montreal, even though their rations had not been resupplied and they knew the British would be waiting for them. General Brown's brigade was tasked with clearing the Canadian shore of the meddlesome militia, and the rest of November 8 was spent ferrying his men and their mounts across the narrow river. It was also the day they learned that the British had a sizable force, the "Corps of Observation," shadowing them on land and water.

There were minor skirmishes along the Canadian shore on the eighth and ninth, but not enough to impede the progress of the flotilla, which reembarked all the troops that had been patrolling the Canadian shore and passed through the Rapide du Plat opposite Hamilton (now called Waddington) without incident. This successful crossing of the second group of rapids may have made the landlubber infantry believe that all the noise about rapids was just that: noise. The more wary boatmen would have almost certainly cautioned, "Wait 'til we get to the Long Sault."

The force traveled eleven miles on the ninth in just a couple of hours due to the swift current. Because of this rapid descent, the flotilla actually got ahead of the land forces of General Brown, so they pulled into shore at Yellow House on the Canadian side to prevent losing the protective cover of the dragoons. Yellow House, as it was called by the Americans, was the farmhouse of a local Canadian militia captain named John Crysler.

On the morning of Wednesday, November 10, Wilkinson waited for word from General Brown that the harassing militia had been dispersed, but the Corps of Observation, just a few miles upstream from him, was not waiting for anything. About a week earlier, Benjamin Richards, the son of Alexander Richards, and a crew of volunteers had captured a convoy of merchant ships headed upriver to Kingston. They were carrying civilian goods only, private property belonging to Kingston merchants Bartlett, Merrills and Badgley.[176] Richards was acting under letters of marque in which any wartime capture is considered fair game.

The goods were taken to Hamilton (Waddington) and stored in a warehouse there, except for some barrels that were carried to Columbia Village (now the village of Madrid), nine miles away. The merchants in Kingston knew who took their goods and where they were stored, so it is a good bet that when the Corps of Observation left Kingston to follow Wilkinson, the merchants might have asked them to try and reclaim their property.

November 10 was cold, wet and windy. When the British landing party arrived at Hamilton, headed by Lieutenant Morrison and Captain Mulcaster of the Royal Navy, David A. Ogden and Alexander Richards were summoned and given an ultimatum: turn over the captured goods immediately or Hamilton would be burned to the ground. The two Americans quickly agreed to show the British where the goods were stored and asked that they spare the village. The British had neither the time nor inclination to go through all the barrels and crates to see what was there or even to take them back to the Canadian side. Morrison and Mulcaster could hear cannon fire downriver from the gunboats and were anxious to get back to their respective commands. Therefore, a capitulation agreement was dictated by which Ogden and Richards swore on their honor that they would load up the goods, including any material belonging to the U.S.

government, and send them across the river to a local Canadian justice of the peace named Jacob Wager, and failing that, they agreed that the village should be destroyed.[177]

As this one-sided negotiation was taking place, Colonel Morrison ordered the burning of the barracks that had been built there at the beginning of the war but spared all the other buildings. With a war to catch up to, the British soon departed and left Ogden and Richards to fulfill their end of the bargain. The capitulation was reported in many newspapers, even if, as in the one below, the name of the village was in error:

> *Another Mishap—We learn from the North that a detachment of the British army, on their way down the river, lately visited Ogdensburg* [i.e. Hamilton] *to look for some English goods and other property on board of seven boats which had been captured by some of our dragoons on the 2nd Instant. After burning the barracks, we understand a capitulation was entered into between the Americans and their invaders, the most important article of which was that the village should remain unmolested on condition that the Americans should send over the seven boats before mentioned, with the prize goods on board, which was done and they departed.*[178]

General Brown had been sent ahead to clear the Canadian shore and to neutralize troops stationed at a blockhouse in Cornwall, which he did admirably well on November 10. Wilkinson needed the Canadian shore as far as the end of the Long Sault rapids completely under his control. This was because his flotilla would have to float down the north channel of the Long Sault one boat at a time, and those single craft would be sitting ducks as they twisted and turned in the churning water, unable to defend themselves if there were troops on the shore just above them ready to attack.

The Corps of Observation had closed in on the rear guard of the flotilla and were occasionally bombarding them from their gunboats and were in intermittent contact with the troops traveling on the King's Highway by the river. The harassment continued all day, and it became a game of cat and mouse, with General Boyd's men getting the worst of it as they would march east a ways, then run west trying to catch up to their tormentors and then march right back over the ground they had just covered. The British would advance close enough to get a few shots off, and the Americans would chase them but never get near enough to actually engage. This went on for much of the day, and by afternoon, the flotilla was fast approaching

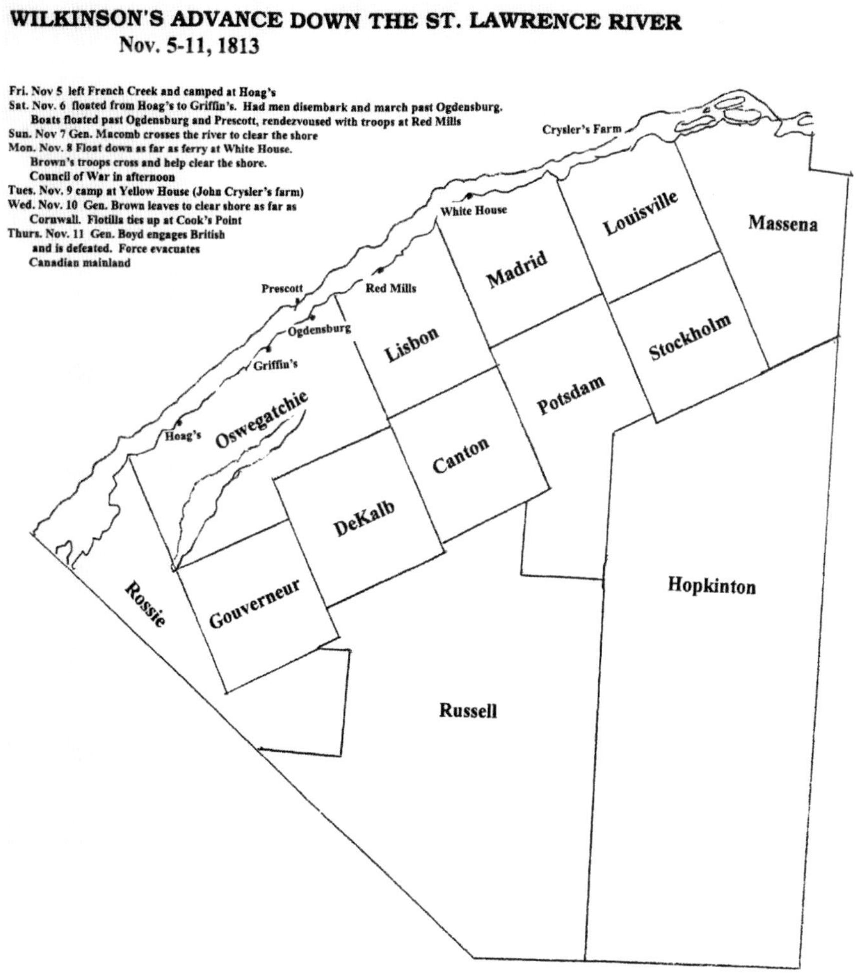

Map showing the stopping places of Wilkinson's expedition down the St. Lawrence.

the Long Sault Rapids, an eight-mile-long roller coaster of white water that would have to be run in daylight. The invading force tied up on the Canadian shore at Cook's Point, just past John Crysler's farm,[179] and spent a miserable night in the cold, rain, sleet and mud. The expedition had traveled only a mile or so all day. Wilkinson was too sick to leave his boat, but the other generals were forced to share the same uncomfortable night as the enlisted men.[180]

November 11 dawned almost as miserable as the tenth and promised to be a repeat of the annoying, unproductive give-and-take that occurred the preceding day, with the only saving grace being that the rain had let up. The Corps of Observation was very close on the heels of Wilkinson's force, separated by only a mile or so of woods and a few gullies, and their gunboats again began their bothersome volleys. Wilkinson did not want to enter the Long Sault until he had heard from General Brown that the coast was clear downriver, since there was no such thing as hoisting the flotilla back up the falls if things went wrong. So they waited much of the day for news from Brown and were occasionally occupied by chasing off the British behind them. General Brown finally sent word that it was safe to proceed, and orders were given to have the flotilla ready at 2:30 p.m. to run the rapids. The infantry had been offloaded and were ready to march downriver, with the U.S. Artillery still on board the boats, along with the food, horses and ammunition.

Colonel Morrison and his 1,200 men may not have had the advantage in numbers, but they had vastly superior leadership and had chosen ground that was perfect for a defensive fight. Morrison had all along broken off any engagement with the Americans because he was so vastly outnumbered. But he had come to a place that was ideally suited for a battle against a superior force and this time did not fall back when General Boyd's troops challenged him. Boyd was inexperienced in combat and showed it: his units were sent in piecemeal and without a resupply of ammunition, which was still on the boats. When it became clear that Morrison would not back down as he had been doing, Boyd called for the artillery, but it took time to unload the cannons from the boats and get them up onto the muddy shore and into place.

There were individual heroics that day, and some men and units performed admirably. General Covington was coolly leading his men against Colonel Pearson when he was struck in the stomach by musket fire and fell mortally wounded, dying the next day on Barnhart Island. However, the overall American performance was amateurish, and the confused, ineffective General Boyd sealed their fate against a foe led by seasoned professionals. A general withdrawal was ordered for the American forces, and once the boats were loaded, the flotilla crossed to the American side of the river just before dark to lick their wounds, abandoning many of the dead and wounded on the field. Some of the dragoons were forced to swim their horses to the other side, a cold and dangerous task. Colonel Morrison had delivered a crushing defeat to a numerically superior foe and forced them to retreat in disarray.

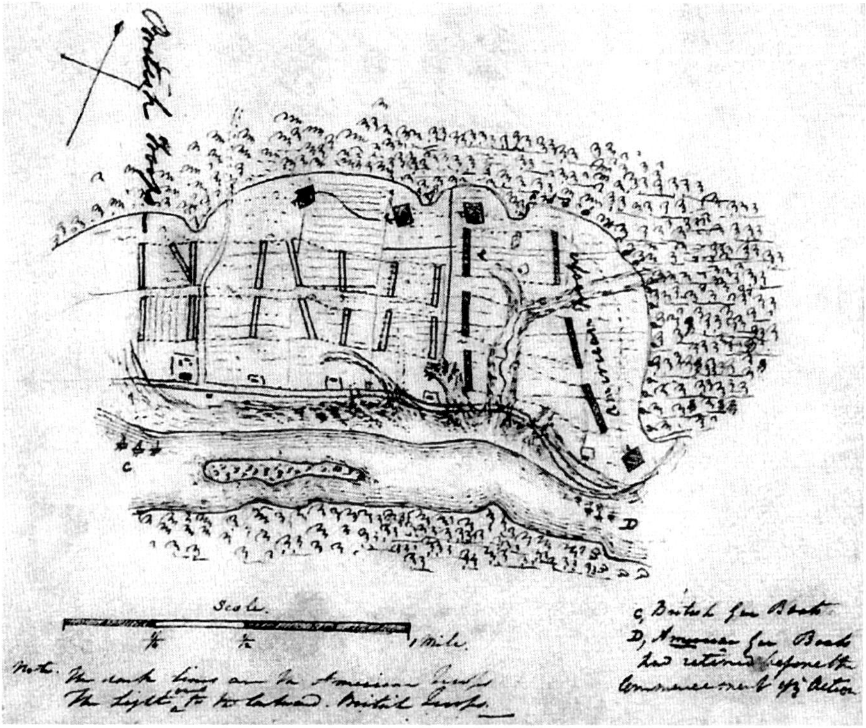

Sketch of the battlefield at Crysler's Farm, November 11, 1813.

The Americans lost 102 men killed, with a further 237 wounded and about 120 captured. The British and Canadians lost only 31 killed, 148 wounded and 9 missing and, of course, forced the Americans off the field.

The next day, November 12, Wilkinson received the news that General Hampton announced that he was not going to rendezvous with him at St. Regis as he had been instructed to do but was instead headed back toward Plattsburgh. Wilkinson used this information to give him an excuse to call off the entire mission. He ordered the flotilla down the American side of the Long Sault rapids and sailed a few more miles until they reached the outlet of the Salmon River. Once there, they rowed six miles up the river to the tiny settlement of French Mills (soon renamed Fort Covington in honor of the slain general) in Franklin County and there set up winter quarters.

Canadian militia captain Reuben Sherwood was not far behind them, and as so often in the past, he provided his superiors with high-quality intelligence.[181] He paid an Irishman named Lynch to get into French Mills and scout out the situation. Lynch reported that the artillery had all been dismounted from the boats and laid on the embankment between the river and the blockhouse. The boats themselves were on shore near the bridge, and one thousand men were engaged in building barracks on both sides of the river.

Thus ended Wilkinson's attempt to capture Montreal, an event the Canadians rightly refer to as "the battle that saved Canada." His defeat at Crysler's Farm is possibly the only reason Montreal is not an American city today.

The Americans pulled the bows of their boats up onto the shore of the Salmon River at French Mills, where the craft promptly became useless, frozen into the ice. The men had no shelter from the bitter winter weather other than tents until the barracks were finished,[182] and disease ravaged those who were lucky enough to make it that far. Death claimed more men in this winter camp than Colonel Morrison's troops did during the battle, while Wilkinson holed up in the palatial home of Richard Harison on Webster Street in Malone. Without any military duties on the near horizon, Wilkinson busied himself by fabricating excuses to explain his failure and fended off attacks on his character and abilities that appeared regularly in the Federalist press. Some of those attacks came from Nathan Ford, who described what he assumed would be Wilkinson's eventual withdrawal to Sackets Harbor "a rather roundabout way of taking Montreal."[183]

With all the suffering of the American troops languishing at French Mills, one would think that the civilian population of the area would step in to help relieve the suffering. Alas, it appears that the same willingness to deal with the British for profit colored the decisions of many men. Smuggling was still a lucrative endeavor, and the British paid top dollar for meat on the hoof. By January 1814, Lieutenant General Gordon Drummond at Kingston could write to Sir George Prevost, "Our supplies for 1,600 men are all drawn from the American side of the river. They drive droves of cattle from the interior under pretense of supplying their own army at the Salmon River and so are allowed to pass the guards and at night to cross them over to our side, the river being frozen. I shall be under the necessity of getting most of my flour from their side."[184]

Chapter 7
OTHER STORIES

THE BARRACKS IN MASSENA AND HAMILTON

The barracks in Massena were constructed in 1812 near present-day Massena Center on the Grasse River. Lieutenant Colonel Thomas Benedict paid a man named Emerson to build them. They were occupied for about ninety days and then abandoned. In September 1813, Major Joseph Anderson of the Stormont County militia attacked the area, burned the barracks and some other buildings nearby and escaped in boats down the Grasse River.

Barracks were being constructed at Hamilton (now Waddington) in July 1812, according to a July 11, 1812 letter from Gouverneur Ogden to his wife, and were burned in the capitulation of Hamilton on November 10, 1813.

BLOCKHOUSES

Blockhouses were built early in the war in Gouverneur, Rossie and Stockholm. The one in Gouverneur was built on Clinton Street in the middle of the road, about halfway down the block, with livery stables on the west and Mr. Francis

M. Holbrook's house on the east side of the road. It took the efforts of most of the men in town to construct it. After the war, the huge spruce timbers from Richville were used in the Oswegatchie dam, and other parts of it, mostly oak, were used in various structures around the village. The following is an accounting of the men who built the blockhouse and how much they contributed. This account was done April 21, 1821. The two women listed are likely to be widows of men who helped, rather than helpers themselves.[185]

Name	Hand Labor Days	Oxen Days
Arnold, Lemuel	6	1
Atwood, Aaron	11	5
Atwood, Joel	8	2
Austin, Colvin P.	9	
Austin, Daniel	3	
Austin, Isaac	30	
Babcock, Pardon	12 ½	
Barnes, Aseph	13	4 ½
Barnes, James	12	
Barnes, Rockwell	29 ½	
Barrell, Collum	12	
Black, Harvey	4	
Bolton, Joseph	4	2
Bowen, Aaron	12	
BrownBenjamin	17	
Brown, John	15	6
Bullock, Calvin	10	4
Carrington, Aaron	11	4
Case, Ephraim	11	
Clark, Oliver	6	
Cleghorn, William	6	
Cole, Eben	2 ½	
Cole, Medad	10	
Cotton, Jonathan	6 ½	1
Crawford, David	7	
Drake, Caleb	5	
Drake, Luther	10	
Foster, William	10	

Name	Hand Labor Days	Oxen Days
Goodrich, Allen	2	
Goodrich, Cheney	9	
Haile, James	7 ½	
Harris, Luther	7	8
Hills, Nathan	12	2
Holbroook, Hnery B.	11	4
Hoyt, John	5	
Kimball, Richard	8	
Kingsley, Jedediah	1	
Laughton, Josiah T.	6	
Leavitt, Benjamin	2	
Marble, Jonathan	8	
Morgan, Isaac	9	5
Nichols, Eleazar	12	6
Noble, Reuben	8	
Parker, Ebenezer	11	
Parker, James	6	6
Patterson, John H.	13	3
Porter, Israel	10	
Rhodes, William P.	13	2
Robinson, Eli	2	
Robinson, Jason	3	
Sackett, Dorothy	10	
Smith, Benjamin	13	8
Smith, Hephen	20	8
Smith, Willard	12	8
Soares, Daniel	7	
Spencer, John	2	2
Thompson, James	10	
Waid, Josiah	3	
Wood, Lydia	8	
Wood, Truman	7	

The blockhouse in the town of Rossie was constructed about halfway between the settlements of Somerville and Wegatchie. It was torn down in 1840.

The Militia Draft

A feeling of near panic swept through the northern parts of New York State in the spring of 1812 when it became clear that the prospect of war was very real. In April 1812, the federal government informed the state governors that they wanted 100,000 men drafted and available for service in case the need arose. Some states, such as Kentucky, had no problems with volunteers, but the northeastern states had a much more difficult time raising troops. New York's quota was 13,500 men,[186] and Governor Tompkins ordered a draft that was conducted on May 5, 1812, in St. Lawrence County, apparently without requiring the men to actually muster.

However, war was declared on June 18, 1812, and the drafted men were held to six months' service: June 26 until December 26, 1812. Most of the drafted men did service in Ogdensburg, but other units were scattered around the county at different times, mostly guarding the shore of the St. Lawrence. When dismissed at Christmas 1812, the militia were not replaced with others, partly because winter warfare was nearly unheard of at that time. One company was drafted in January 1813 to serve at Ogdensburg for three months, but the majority of militia members never served again after the capture of Ogdensburg in February 1813.

Opposition to the war was so high in many parts of the county that many men did not respond to the militia draft. Assemblyman Roswell Hopkins said that his constituents "in every town I have heard from, have manifested a determination to resist [the draft] peaceably if they could but forcibly if they must."[187]

The *Northern Whig* carried a story in January 1814, not long after the disaster at Chrysler's Farm, concerning a bill in the House of Representatives to increase the pay of a common soldier to $10.00 per month and to increase the enlistment bounty to $100.00. The paper decried the $21 million that this would cost for a year and stated that "the necessity of offering such extravagant wages to the common soldier is indubitable evidence of the hostility of the people to this unhallowed war."[188] Militia privates made $6.66 a month during most of the war, which was not enough to cover the cost of replacing their labor on their farms.

The Battle of Toussaint's Island

Because control of the American side of the river was in the hands of local militiamen, there was never any overall strategic plan as to how to proceed with the war or even *whether* to proceed with the war. The opposing forces were only a few thousand feet apart, and many small skirmishes occurred, more by random provocation than by any grand strategic design. An example of such a confrontation was the gun battle at Toussaint's Island[189] on September 15, 1812.

Toussaint's Island was a fairly large island right in the middle of a very narrow part of the channel, about halfway between Red Mills and Iroquois Point in the town of Lisbon.[190] Just north of Toussaint's Island was a smaller island named Presqu'ile. The two islands forced the waters of the St. Lawrence into very narrow channels, ideal for an ambush.

A convoy of thirty-three British boats, commanded by James Fitzgibbon (who later accepted the American surrender at Beaver Dams), was under the escort of a detachment of the Newfoundland Regiment commanded by Major Rowland Heathcote and a flank company of the Dundas Militia under Captain Michael Ault. This convoy was on its way from Montreal to Kingston, laden with military stores. American observers spotted the flotilla and reported their presence to the military command upriver at Ogdensburg.

Colonel Thomas Benedict, commanding at Ogdensburg, ordered Major Martin Nash and his seventy men to march upriver about eight miles and get over to Toussaint's Island at "the Narrows" and attack the boats from there. Meanwhile, Major Richard Flack commanded another party composed of a gunboat under the command of Adjutant Daniel Church and two Durham boats under the command of Captain Elisha Griffin. Church's gunboat had a crew of eighteen and a single six-pound cannon mounted on it. Their mission was to try and intercept the flotilla in the neighborhood of Toussaint's Island and capture whatever goods it might have to offer.

That night, the American force floated down the river and made camp on the American shore opposite Toussaint's Island. Before sunrise, this party had taken up a position on Toussaint's Island and had the gunboat stationed at the foot of the island. The Americans had captured Mr. Toussaint, whose home was on the island, as a precaution, lest he alert the British to the ambush as they approached the narrows. However, just as the British boats approached, Mr. Toussaint escaped his captors and was able to row a canoe out to warn the British.

Having been apprised of the danger, the convoy stopped and off-loaded some of the troops so that they could advance up the shore and cover the flotilla as it neared Presqu'ile. Major Heathcote had made preparations to defend the boats in case the enemy decided to attack at that vulnerable spot. Ensign Clark and part of Captain Ault's company were ferried across to Presqu'ile and got to the south side of that small island just as two American vessels filled with troops were preparing to land. Clark's party, camouflaged by trees and bushes, suddenly opened fire on them, and with enough effect the Americans immediately retreated back to Toussaint's Island, where they took shelter in the woods. In their haste and confusion, one of their boats went adrift and was picked up downstream by the Canadians; it contained seven muskets, two swords and a quantity of provisions.[191]

With the element of surprise lost and one of their boats captured, the situation did not look good for the Americans. The fighting lasted until about 11:00 a.m., and the Americans finally broke off the engagement, just as Canadian militia and a gunboat from upriver were joining in the fight. In a short time, a large number of the inhabitants from different parts of the county were assembled on Presqu'ile, among them Captain Ault, Captain Shaver and Colonel Allan Macdonell, who was commanding the Dundas Militia. Two companies of the Grenville Militia under Captains Hugh Monro and Philip Dulmage also arrived, and a nine-pound cannon that had been captured from the French at Chimney Island in 1760 was brought from Prescott by Lieutenant Richard D. Fraser.

All told, the Americans lost one bateau in the fray and three men wounded, one of whom, Joseph McComber, later died and was buried on the American shore.[192] A deserter told the Americans that twelve British were killed on the spot, and seven more died the next day. There were also forty wounded. The British records do not list anywhere near this number of casualties.

About three weeks later, Major Rowland Heathcote submitted his official report of the engagement to Colonel Vincent:

> *Sir,*
>
> *I have the honor to report for the information of Major General Brock that at ½ past seven o'clock in the morning of the 10th ultimo, as the brigade of boats under my command entered the narrow passage between Presque'ile* [sic] *and an island known by the name of Toussaint's, the enemy who were concealed in the wood in number we supposed between three and four hundred opened a brisk fire of musketry from one extremity of the island*

> *to the other on the batteaux. The detachment was immediately landed and formed in the best manner to protect the stores and repel the attack of the enemy by returning a well-directed and spirited fire.*
>
> *At this moment, a schooner carrying a six-pounder came round the lower point of the island and commenced firing upon us with round shot which was continued about an hour. At the same time, a large durham boat filled with men came round the upper point of the island, apparently with the intention of landing upon Presque'ile, in consequence of which I ordered a party consisting of about 30 of the detachment and a number of militia to proceed to the point opposite the durham boat, and I have the satisfaction to state that their fire was so well directed that the enemy were driven from the point and the boat taken possession of. The schooner shortly after this hauled around to the back of the island and with the assistance of several boats conveyed the men from the island to the main shore. I then proceeded with the batteaux and passed the narrows and rapids, the enemy continuing to fire from their own shore but at too great a distance to do execution.*
>
> *The gunboat which Col. Lethbridge had ordered from Prescott having arrived, the American schooner got under way and from superiority of sailing escaped the* [illegible]. *I have every reason to be perfectly satisfied with the conduct of the officers and men of the detachment under my command. I have also to acknowledge the assistance I received from the militia who readily came forward to render every service of their power. I have to report that one private of the 49th Regt. was killed by a cannon shot, and one private of the Newfoundland Regt. and one or two of the militia slightly wounded. From the information I received, the enemy must have suffered considerably on their occasion.*[193]

Samuel Stacy Jr. and Habeas Corpus

Loring Austin and George Wells were not the only military officers who overstepped the bounds of jurisprudence. On June 30, 1813, Samuel Stacy Jr. of Madrid was taken into custody by a Captain Smith at Watertown as he was on his way from Sackets Harbor back to Madrid. This was done on the orders of Commodore Isaac Chauncey, commander of the American fleet on Lake Ontario. Stacy was accused of being a spy for the British, having been at Sackets Harbor and asking questions concerning the troops and the fleet then at anchor there. Upon arrival at Sackets, he was placed under arrest in a tent and was apparently never informed of the charges against him. He became ill and was housed in another building, again under close confinement and armed guard.

When a writ of habeas corpus was served on General Morgan Lewis, army commander at Sackets Harbor, by Nathan Williams, a commissioner of the New York State Supreme Court, Lewis returned the writ, saying that Stacy was not "in my custody." That statement was technically true enough, but it was intentionally misleading. General Lewis was saying that he *personally* did not have custody of Stacy, which, of course, was true. However, officers under his command *did* have Stacy under guard there at Sackets Harbor. A different scenario was played out when Royal Torrey,[194] provost marshal at Sackets Harbor, was served with the writ. He admitted that he had Stacy and enclosed a copy of his orders from John Chambers, the assistant adjutant general:

> *Sir,*
>
> *You will receive into the custody of the provost guard, from Commodore Chauncey, Samuel Stacy, charged by him, the said Commodore, with an act of high treason against the government of the United States, committed within the territory of the King of Great Britain.*

When questioned about Stacy's detention, Captain Smith wrote that Stacy was "arrested by a verbal order from Commodore Chauncey, and under suspicion, as he believed, of having connection in some way with the enemy." Jefferson County sheriff Justin Butterfield was successful in rooting out the fact that Stacy was indeed in custody at Sackets Harbor, whether any high-ranking officer would admit it or not. General Lewis informed him that Stacy had been giving information to the British and was involved in other treasonable practices and that a court martial was the proper venue for a trial.

Chief Justice James Kent of the New York State Supreme Court of Judicature decided that Stacy must be set free and tried in a civilian court if warranted. The court mentioned that habeas corpus was the "glory of the English law." The court further stated that General Lewis was not the military commander of the citizens of the United States, but only of its soldiers.

The following is Commodore Chauncey's letter to Secretary of the Navy William Jones concerning the recent arrest of Stacy:

U.S. Ship Madison, Sacket's Harbor, July 4, 1813
To The Honorable William Jones, Secretary of the Navy, Washington

Sir: On the 1st instant, I caused Mr. Samuel Stacey to be apprehended as a spy. Mr. Stacey lives upon the St. Lawrence, a few miles below Ogdensburg, and I have the most positive information that he has been in the habit of conveying information to the enemy for many months. He visited this place a few days before the British made the attack on the 29th of May, and I have no doubt but that he is the person that gave the information that most of the troops had been sent to Niagara. I had information from the person that I employ on the other side that this man would visit the Harbor about the last of June. He was accordingly watched. When he left Ogdensburg, he said he was going to Utica upon important business. He told others that he was going into the Western country to collect money, instead of which, he came to the Harbor, without any ostensible business, and made a great many inquiries respecting the fleet; when they would sail? and the force of the new ship? &c &c. I therefore thought it my duty to detain this man for trial. I can prove his frequent intercourse with the enemy. At any rate, I shall deprive the enemy of the information which he could have conveyed to him, which is all important at this time.

It would be very desirable to hang this traitor to his country, as he is considered respectable in the country in which he lives; and I think that it is full time to make an example of some of our countrymen who are so base and degenerate as to betray their country by becoming the spies and informers of our enemy. I hope the steps which I have taken, with respect to Mr. Stacey, will meet with your approbation. I have the honor to be, very respectfully, sir, your obedient servant, Isaac Chauncey.

The Secretary of War ordered Stacy released because, as he put it, "a citizen cannot be considered as a spy." Everyone is entitled to his opinion, including Captain Reuben Sherwood of the Canadian militia, himself an accomplished spy, who later wrote:

I hereby certify that the bearer, Mr. Saml. Stacy, was employed by Lt. Col. Pearson in Secret Service in the summer of 1813—and that I was several times sent to him for particular information during that summer and fall.

Canadian militia captain Paul Glasford echoed those sentiments a few months later when he wrote:

> *I hereby certify that the bearer hereof, Mr. Samuel Stacy, was engaged by Lt. Col. Pearson and Lt. Col MacDonell commanding at Ft. Wellington from the first of March 1813 to the first of March 1815 in Secret Service on several important occasions and that much important information of the state and movements of the American armies was from time to time communicated to Lt. Col. MacDonell and Col. Pearson respectively. I frequently brought him personally before Col. Pearson to give the information personally, and I am well informed of his suffering about six weeks imprisonment at Sackets Harbor on the same account for his services previous to that of his confinement at the harbor. He always received through my hands the stipulated sums agreed for, but I have no knowledge of his receiving anything on account of his suffering imprisonment nor for the services he rendered afterwards in going to the Four Corners* [i.e. Chateaugay, NY] *and several other places during the winter of 1814—but I have several times heard Col. Pearson say he should be handsomely rewarded for his suffering and service.*[195]

Stacy went through great lengths after the war to get compensated for his imprisonment at Sackets Harbor, and he had great help in that regard from benefactors no less than Lieutenant Colonel George MacDonell, who credited Stacy with providing Sir George Prevost with the intelligence that convinced him to attack Sackets Harbor in 1813.[196]

"Pressing" Teams

Although it may seem like a trivial complaint compared to some men getting shot or dying of disease, the practice of impressing (or "pressing," as it was usually called) was not limited to men in the navy, nor was it limited to the British as perpetrators. "Pressing" in this case refers to the practice of U.S. Army or militia soldiers taking horses, oxen, sleighs or wagons of some kind for their use, without permission and without compensating their owners. When General James Wilkinson slunk away from Crysler's Farm in November 1813, he established himself in the Harison mansion on Webster Street in Malone while the remnants of his army lived like dogs in the frozen wasteland of French Mills. By the end of February 1814, some of the men had been ordered to Sackets Harbor under General Brown, and the rest of the army was sent to Plattsburgh. It is a long walk from French Mills to anywhere, so the army scoured the surrounding countryside and appropriated almost any beast of burden they could find and all the sleighs that were road worthy.[197] In this manner, several thousand men were transported hundreds of miles in the dead of winter through an almost trackless winter wilderness. There are many newspaper accounts of teams and sleighs being taken by force. Not only that, but food for animals and humans was also confiscated in the name of the U.S. government.

THE RICHARDS FAMILY IN THE MIDDLE OF IT

Canadian Samuel Adams of Edwardsburgh in Dundas County had volunteered to do service in Captain William Fraser's company of Light Dragoons on the morning of November 11, 1813, realizing that the cat-and-mouse game the Americans were playing with the British could not go on forever. He had not yet been given any specific duties and so apparently decided to go on a fact-finding mission of his own in the area loosely watched by the American pickets near John Crysler's farm. As he was secreting himself in the woods, he spied two American officers from the Fifteenth U.S. Infantry Regiment—Captain White Young and Captain Charles Bruce—walking along with no escort and no weapons drawn. He emerged from hiding and captured the two, who concluded erroneously that the musket being leveled at them was loaded.[198] Within a few minutes, both officers were brought before the British commander and signed parole agreements. As part of the bargain, they were to be taken to Prescott, so as to be out of the way when and if an actual engagement flared up.

As mentioned in a previous chapter, the village of Hamilton had capitulated to the British the day before and agreed to surrender all the commercial goods that had been captured from the merchants at Kingston and subsequently stored in Hamilton. In fulfillment of this agreement, Alexander Richards accompanied the boats laden with the goods to the Canadian shore about seven miles downriver on the same day, November 11, 1813. He landed near Zephrinus Casselman's tavern in Williamsburg, not even a half mile from where a battle would be raging within just a few hours. He was there presumably looking for Jacob Wager, a justice of the peace, so that he could turn over the goods to him and be gone before things got out of hand. He was certainly aware that he was in a dangerous situation, with British and American forces within sight of each other. However, he had no choice but to be there—he did not doubt for a minute that the British would return to Hamilton and burn it down if he failed to fulfill his part of the capitulation.

So there he was at Casselman's when two armed men came into the tavern, accompanied by Captain White Young, who as a prisoner of war was being escorted upriver to Prescott. The two guards refreshed themselves at the tavern and then left with their prisoner, headed down to the shore. Apparently, within a few minutes of their boat getting upstream of the British gunships, it was spotted by Alexander Richards's two sons, Ben and Alex Jr., plus John Carty, in a boat of their own. The Americans did not have any idea what was going on exactly, but they did not have to be told that a U.S. Army officer sitting in a boat under guard and headed upriver meant trouble. Without any hesitation, the Americans overtook the Canadians and took control of their craft. Ben Richards was used to doing this sort of thing, as he was the one who captured the British goods in the first place. In any event, the three Americans brought the guards and their prisoner back to Hamilton on the New York side, where they promptly set Captain Young free. They disarmed the guards but would not take them back to the Canadian side, claiming their boat was too small.[199]

By not having himself transported back into British hands, Captain Young had violated the terms of his military parole, in which he swore on his honor not to take part in any offensive actions but to stay in Canada under supervision until he could be exchanged for a British POW of equal rank. On November 14, 1813, British colonel John Harvey sent the indispensible Captain William Gilkison to the U.S. Army camp at French Mills (now Fort Covington) complaining that Captains Young and Bruce had violated their paroles and asking for official explanation or redress. He also sought damages and an explanation for what he termed "that system of rapine and plundering of the property of the peaceful and unoffending inhabitants which has marked the progress of the American army during its short continuance in this province."[200]

Colonel John Walbach, the American adjutant general, replied the same day.[201] In his reply, he basically said that the United States adhered to the laws of war and that he would look into the alleged parole violation, as well as the reports of American troops plundering Canadian homes. It appears that the two captains never did go back to Canada to fulfill the obligations of their parole.

Madrid Revisited

When the village of Hamilton capitulated in November 1813, it was known at the time that not all the goods captured from Kingston merchants had been recovered. The British planned and executed a second incursion to recover the rest of the merchandise captured by Benjamin Richards under a letter of marque the previous fall. British records reveal that not only were there goods secreted in Columbia Village (now Madrid Village) but that the American government had also advertized them for sale.[202]

This British raid occurred on February 6, 1814, and troops involved included a subaltern, two sergeants and twenty rank and file of the Royal Marines, plus ten soldiers of the Incorporated Militia of Prescott under the command of Captains John Kerr and Reuben Sherwood.[203]

Reuben Sherwood was one of the most successful Canadian spies during the war. He had had intimate knowledge of much of St. Lawrence County before the war and was apparently able to move through the county at any time without fear of being recognized or challenged. Sherwood knew where Columbia Village was and acted as the guide for the expedition.

Once Kerr, Sherwood and their men crossed the St. Lawrence, they impressed horses and sleighs and went directly to Columbia Village, eight miles away on the Grasse River. They got to the storehouse and loaded the goods by around 4:30 the next morning, but they were forced to leave at least twenty sleigh loads for lack of transport. They then rode back up to Hamilton and loaded the boats waiting for them there under the direction of Lieutenant Shaver of the Dundas militia.

Hough claims that the party engaged in this incursion returned about daylight, decked out with ribbons and streamers of brilliant colors, which formed a part of their capture, and recrossed the St. Lawrence without the loss of a man. He also states that a group of men was formed to try and recover the goods but that a quantity of "shrub" liquor was left in a conspicuous place and that the pursuing party decided to partake of it rather than to stir up more trouble.[204]

It is interesting to note that although the goods were recaptured and would normally have been evaluated and prize money split among the party, the merchandise had been wet and damaged and when brought to Montreal was auctioned for a pittance of its original worth, £260. As late as 1819, Kerr and Sherwood were asking the governor general of Canada to intercede for them and get them their share of the booty.[205]

The Raid at Hopkinton

Eight weeks after their defeat at Crysler's Farm, the surviving troops of Wilkinson's corps were still holed up in French Mills and Malone, slowly dying of disease and exposure. Having the entire northern army bivouacked in the frozen wilderness made no military or humanitarian sense whatsoever. Therefore, in January 1814, Secretary of War John Armstrong ordered Wilkinson, who was then quite comfy in Richard Harison's house on Webster Street in Malone, to have General Jacob Brown take two thousand of the remaining soldiers back to Sackets Harbor whence they came and to have the rest of the army trudge eastward to Plattsburgh, where they would spend the rest of the winter.

One of the main problems with having so many men in northern Franklin County was the difficulty of keeping them supplied with food and medicine. Long convoys of sleighs were constantly on the move from east and west trying to keep up with the demand for food, supplies and medicine at French Mills. However, once the order to leave French Mills was received, it was not clear what should be done with supply trains that were currently en route.

On February 2, 1814, John Gilbert arrived in Hopkinton with orders from General Swartout, quartermaster general at French Mills, stating that all flour and other public property on its way to French Mills from Sackets Harbor should be halted there at Hopkinton and stored until further notice. This made sense, since the army was leaving French Mills as fast as it could. There were about three hundred barrels of flour and several hundred bushels of oats and corn. The provisions were stored in a barn on Judge Hopkins's farm, which was then occupied by a Dr. Sprague, and the teams were sent on, relieved of their burdens, to French Mills in order to provide transportation for the evacuation of some of the troops and their equipment.

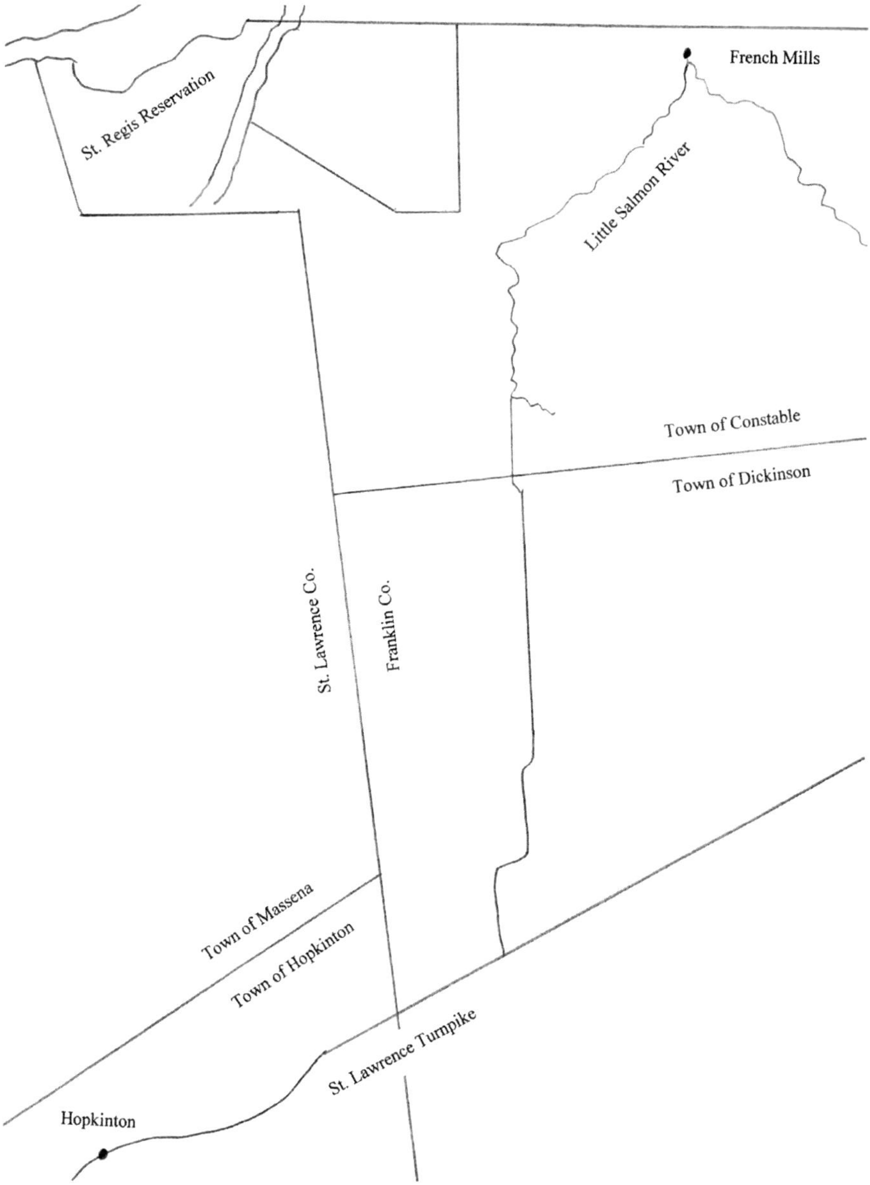

Map of the route taken by the British on the Hopkinton raid in February 1814.

On February 12, six sleds bearing eighteen-pound cannons arrived in Hopkinton from French Mills on their way to Sackets Harbor. The oxen were completely worn out (each cannon weighed almost two tons), and so fresh local oxen were procured to continue the journey. On February 14, the assistant quartermaster general was in Hopkinton, and local men offered to use their own teams and spans of oxen to remove the flour back to Sackets for safe keeping, since it would obviously not be needed in French Mills. This they proposed to do for either cash or a percentage of the cargo. Their motives were at least partially self-serving, as the hidden stores might very well bring British trouble down on their heads once the protection of the American army vanished. The officer declined their offer, saying that he did not have the authority to move the flour anywhere.

The troops were evacuating French Mills by February 7, and by February 15, the Ninth, Twenty-fifth, Eleventh and Twenty-first Regiments of Infantry, in that order, as well as the Third Artillery, had passed through Hopkinton on their way to Sackets Harbor without so much as a glance at the provisions still stored there in Hopkins's barn.

The last of the troops left French Mills on February 13, burning most of the remaining tents and supplies and all 328 of the surviving boats of Wilkinson's November flotilla. They also burned the barracks and cut the masts of the remaining boats[206] as a parting gesture. The next day, a British force of 1,300 men commanded by Colonel Hercules Scott sailed up the Salmon River and landed at French Mills. They were composed mostly of the 103rd and 89th Foot but also included some artillery, dragoons, fencibles and elements of the Glengarry and Stormont militias. Lieutenant Colonel Joseph Morrison, who had led the force that dogged Wilkinson on his way down the river, was second in command. On the same morning, General Jacob Brown himself showed up at French Mills, accompanied by a Colonel Gaines and the press master (the man responsible for impressing civilian owned teams and sleighs). They had left Malone and were on their way to Sackets Harbor via Russell. They arrived at the abandoned cantonment and left almost immediately, apparently just missing being captured by the British.

The British set up camp at French Mills and scoured the place for any supplies or equipment that had escaped the American torch. At the end of the week, Colonel Scott split his force into several raiding parties and had them scout the area for any materiel worth sending back to Canada. They raided Malone on February 19 and then turned their attention to Chateaugay, returning again to French Mills on the twenty-first with upward of five hundred sleighs full of captured provisions and equipment.[207]

It appears that an American spy had informed Scott's officers that there was a large quantity of food hidden in Hopkinton and that it was there for the taking. Major Peter William de Haren[208] and Lieutenant Charlton were dispatched by Colonel Scott with enough men of the 103rd Regiment of Foot and sleighs to raid Hopkinton and capture the provisions. Thus, on the night of February 21, 1814, De Haren and his raiding party set out for Hopkinton. They followed the Salmon River up to the present-day village of Bombay and then straight south to the turnpike and on into the village, where they arrived unnoticed at about 6:30 a.m. on February 22, the first anniversary of the capture of Ogdensburg.

As expected, there was no military force of any kind and no guards protecting the supplies. Sentries were posted at each house to prevent mischief, and as much of the provisions as their sleighs could carry were loaded up and made ready for the twenty-seven-mile journey back to French Mills. There was not room enough for all 289 barrels, so the British proposed burning the excess, approximately 90 barrels, but were implored by the residents to let them buy the extra. This the British agreed to, stipulating that the villagers had to swear that none of the flour would be given to the army, on pain of having it destroyed, along with the barn it had been stored in.

With that, the raiders got back in their sleighs and headed for their encampment at French Mills. They soon left that place and returned with their booty to Canada.[209] As Nathan Ford remarked, "Why provisions should be brought to a retreating army when that same army was destroying a large quantity of surplus provision is a question not easy to solve upon rational principles."[210]

RAIDS ON ROSSIE

In 1814, the areas now known as Hammond, Rossie and a part of Fowler were still all one large town known as Rossie. The northern edge of the town bordered the St. Lawrence River, and the southern parts contained some very rough, rocky ground, mostly still unoccupied and with few roads. The combination of nearness to Canada and the difficulty moving around made the Rossie of 1814 a perfect base of operations for any man or gang of men who felt that horse stealing was a proper way to make a living, and reportedly, there was no shortage of such men.

The ruins of the Rossie Iron Furnace as they looked in the early part of the twentieth century. *Courtesy of the St. Lawrence County Historical Association.*

Horse thieves were equal-opportunity predators and cared little whether they stole Canadian or American horses as long as they could hide their prizes in the wilderness for a few weeks undetected and then sell them for a large profit. The American victims in the area would certainly have liked to see the thieves caught and prosecuted, but the St. Lawrence County sheriff would have only had a few men to help patrol an immense land area, so the odds of chasing down and arresting these men were not good. However, this was wartime, and the British on the other side of the river considered horse theft not only a felony but also an act of war. Accordingly, they acted at least twice to apprehend men they believed to be responsible for crimes of several types, including horse theft.

One such incursion took place in the summer of 1814. A man was believed to have committed some sort of crimes in Canada when he lived there and then fled across the river to escape capture. Duncan Fraser led a party of about fifty or sixty militia across the river to try and effect his capture. They crossed at Chippewa Bay and tried to make their way to Jeduthan Barker's tavern, about one mile south of Hammond on the Ogdensburg Turnpike. However, they lost their way, and by the time they got to the tavern, the man had been aroused from his slumber and escaped, partially clothed but fully alive.[211]

The next British invasion was also apparently in the summer of 1814 (although some sources say 1813), and this raid was again led by a Fraser—this time, Thomas Fraser. They came to Rossie village and stayed in Horatio Berthrong's hotel. They were not successful in locating any thieves but apparently inspected Parish's blast furnace to make sure it was not making munitions. The next day, they returned to Brockville empty-handed.

Nathan Ford at It Again

Not all forms of warfare are violent. Certain belligerent actions have a wider, more pernicious goal than simply winning a battle. One example of such warfare is economic warfare, in which one country tries to damage the economy of the other. A bankrupt country cannot pay for its war materiel or military payroll, and the resulting economic chaos sours the inhabitants against the government either because of the scarcity of goods or because of runaway inflation or both.

One method of attacking the economy of an adversary is counterfeiting their currency, which acts to lower the confidence of the people in their government and may require the government to take expensive measures such as designing, minting and distributing new currency.

So, the concept of one nation aiding and abetting the counterfeiters of an adversary is a legitimate war aim, one that may produce serious consequences for the targeted country. Nathan Ford, always pro-British in his politics, knew of a skilled counterfeiter living near Brockville who had produced plates with which he could simulate British Army scrip. Ford's first instinct was to alert his British friends of the scheme and hope that they could find and punish the villain. A true American patriot would have wished the counterfeiter well, since his success would ultimately hurt the British cause. But Nathan Ford wanted to prove his value to the British who kept an eye on his village, so he informed the authorities in Prescott and let them do their best detective work. He may have also had some sort of personal motive for wanting the man captured, as it is possible that he had been active on the American side of the river as well. On June 27, 1813, Ford wrote the following to Colonel Thomas Pearson:

Co . Pearson
27 June 1813

Dear Sir,

I have reason to believe there is a scheme formed for counterfeiting your paper. You have a number of our old counterfeiters among you—they are equal to the villainy. There is a man by the name of Tabiather Boice who lives back of Brockville. I think if a plan is formed with sufficient secrecy, he will be found not only with much of the paper, but also the plate. There has [sic] *a man left your country I understand to procure assistance, either to have a parcel struck off or to procure paper. And from what I have been informed, this Boice is at the bottom of it. If I get further information of those villains, I will let you know. It is hardly necessary for me to request you will destroy this as soon as you read it.*

However, instead of destroying the letter, Colonel Pearson sent it on to Colonel Edward Baynes, the adjutant general of Canada. He wrote:

Prescott
June 30, 1813

Sir,

I take the liberty of providing the enclosed letter for His Excellency's information and to request his further instructions for my guidance. The man in question, Boyce [sic], *after much difficulty I have succeeded in taking, and he is now a close prisoner at Prescott. He bears the most infamous character* [illegible] *kind of villainy of any man in this country and is the acknowledged leader of a gang who* [infect/infest] *this country and possess a constant patronage with the Americans. From what I can hear, their present business of counterfeiting is supposed by some people on the opposite shore to be with the connivance of the American government. It has been hinted to be the case, but not directly reported as a fact. My informant is Judge Ford, whose name must of course be buried in our own breasts, and too much caution cannot be observed in the treatment of this fellow to prevent a suspicion of where my information comes respecting him. I have still people on the look out for others who are concerned in this business,*

> *and I am in hopes I shall succeed in making some discoveries. Nothing was to be found in this fellow's house, and I am now closely watching the man with whom he constantly* [illegible] *and with whom it is understood he is closely connected. I am sorry to say that my attention is too much occupied with men of this description who are inhabitants of this part of my district. I have traced the robbing of the batteau below Hamilton to have been committed by two or more of our own people. They are presently known, and I hope in a few days to have possession of their persons with such documents as will temporarily lead to their* [illegible].[212]

A man named Reuben Ainsworth was arrested in Cornwall in the fall of 1813 for passing a counterfeit army bill for twenty-five dollars. At the same time, it was discovered that counterfeit (British) army bills for one, four and twenty-five dollars were being publicly offered for sale in Ogdensburg and that "disaffected" (i.e. disloyal or at least unenthusiastic) Canadians who were from the United States, especially those living in the Johnstown district, would cross the river to get the fake bills and put them in circulation. The situation was so bad that General de Rottenburg declared martial law in the Johnstown district because so many farmers refused to sell hay, potatoes and other provisions to the British army. Martial law was revoked two months later.

In February 1814, Colonel Pearson at Prescott found out that trading licenses with the United States were being used to introduce agents of the enemy (America) into the strongly disaffected areas of Leeds and Grenville and Bastard and that these agents brought back intelligence about all the British movements and military dispositions. Accordingly, he cancelled the licenses to stop the espionage

Colonel Baynes, the British adjutant general, said that the area between Kingston and Cornwall was so full of these disaffected Canadians that if it were not for the Scottish settlers in Glengarry and Stormont, communication between Kingston and Cornwall would not have been secure.

On October 25, 1813, William Gilkison of Prescott wrote a warning letter to Colonel Pearson stating that a "friend" in Ogdensburg, almost certainly Ford, had told him about a gang that was counterfeiting British army bills and that one of the gang had gone to Utica to get a fresh supply.[213]

NOTES

CHAPTER 1

1. The Presbyterian Nathan Ford himself being an exception.
2. It seems that the Democratic-Republicans mostly referred to themselves as "Republicans," whereas the Federalists—at least in St. Lawrence County—tended to call them "Democrats," among other things.
3. Strum, "Property Qualifications and Voting Behavior," 362.
4. For example, he wrote to the local assemblyman, "I observe in your letter to Mr. Hasbrouck that D.A.O. [David A. Ogden] is to be appointed one of our judges. This I should not be surprised to see, for he began more than a year ago to kiss DeWitt's backside—he is no doubt a good democrat." (Letter from Nathan Ford to Roswell Hopkins, March 9, 1812.) Ford's poor spelling should not be confused with a poor intellect. His letters to his brother reveal an extremely keen mind and an ironclad grasp of the political and military realities of the day. He was nobody's fool, as Alexander Richards later learned to his regret. As Ford aged, he became, if anything, more combative and profane.
5. Captain Benjamin Forsyth was the U.S. commander during the capture of Ogdensburg.
6. Nathan Ford to David Ford, March 10, 1813.

7. John Ross to David Parish, March 27, 1813.
8. John Ross to David Parish, April 3, 1813.
9. John Ross to David Parish, March 6, 1813.
10. Dispatch from Noah Freer to George Prevost, June 18, 1813. RG 8 C-3527, vol. 1221, 169. National Archives of Canada.
11. John Ross to David Parish, March 27, 1813.
12. Louis Hasbrouck to his wife, May 7, 1813.
13. Nathan Ford to David Ford, September 2, 1813.
14. Nathan Ford to Colonel Thomas Pearson, June 27, 1813.
15. Letters to and from William Gilkison and the commissary general at Prescott, December 9, 1813. National Archives of Canada, M-3526, vol. 1221, 10–11. General Drummond himself gave his blessings to the operation a few weeks later, as long as it produced the required provisions. See National Archives of Canada, RG 8 M-3527, vol. 1221, 282.
16. John Ross to David Parish, October 9, 1814. As a matter of fact, Ross had ingratiated himself so much with the British that he bragged in an October 15 letter to Parish that he could travel in Canada as he pleased, "without the tedious formalities of obtaining a passport." At the time, he was trying to have himself certified as a "neutral." See letters from John Ross to David Parish, November 20, 1814, and November 27, 1814.
17. Nathan Ford to David Ford, June 5, 1814.
18. Nathan Ford to David Ford, November 5, 1813.
19. Nathan Ford to David Ford, September 10, 1813.
20. *Saratoga Patriot*, December 28, 1813, 3.
21. French Mills was the original name of Fort Covington, New York, a small village on the Little Salmon River in Franklin County. Wilkinson's army retreated there after its defeat at Crysler's Farm in November 1813.
22. Whether true or not, it was widely believed that some local citizen had betrayed the location of the hidden mortars, and it was even reported as such in the *Kingston Gazette* of November 13, 1813.
23. *National Intelligencer*, "Calumny Exposed," November 30, 1813. Reprinted in the *American Watchman* on January 8, 1814.
24. See the January 13, 1814 issue of the *New York Herald* for David Ford's defense of his brother, sent to the *New York Evening Post* and the *National Intelligencer* from his home in Morristown, New Jersey. In a February 16, 1814 letter to his brother, Nathan Ford mentions that he is being sued by Wilkinson.
25. A Northhampton farmer quoted in the February 9, 1814 edition of the *True American*.

26. *The Columbian*, December 31, 1813, 2.
27. *New York Evening Post*, January 26, 1814.
28. Joseph Rosseel to David Parish, January 26, 1814. "I was in Ogdensburgh last Monday morning when our Judge and Shepherd was by the marshal translated to New York to stand trial."
29. *Ontario Repository*, February 15, 1814; Northern Whig, February 3, 1814. The *Northern Whig* reported that the charges of high treason had been brought against Ford by two British deserters.
30. *Cooperstown Federalist*, January 29, 1814.
31. *New Hampshire Sentinel*, February 12, 1814.
32. Extract of a letter printed on February 19, 1814, in the *New York Herald*. Italics are original.
33. Nathan Ford to David Ford, February 16, 1814.
34. Nathan Ford to David Ford, October 30, 1814.
35. Nathan Ford to David Ford, September 3, 1814.

Chapter 2

36. David Parish to Joseph Rosseel, April 24, 1809.
37. Joseph Rosseel to David Parish, June 13, 1809.
38. Joseph Rosseel to David Parish, January 18, 1809, and March 7, 1809.
39. Joseph Rosseel to David Parish, July 11, 1809.
40. February 4, 1811 entry in the Parish ledger book at Ogdensburg Public Library. Christian Holmes of Sweden was the captain of the *Experiment*, while Samuel Dixon sailed the *Collector*. Parish named the ship *Collector* after one of the ships he employed to move Spanish bullion from Mexico.
41. Swe-kat-si Chapter of the DAR, *Reminiscences of Ogdensburg*, 169. Captain Obed Mayo was the nautical expert in Ogdensburg and had his own ship, the *Genesee Packet*, built at Ogdensburg in 1810.
42. David Parish to Joseph Rosseel, June 28, 1809.
43. Joseph Rosseel to David Parish, July 5, 1810.
44. David Parish to Secretary of the Navy Paul Hamilton, June 21, 1812.
45. The *Growler* was captured by the British in 1813 and then recaptured a few months later. It was again captured by the British and renamed the HMS *Hamilton*, which is apparently how it ended its career. The *Collector* was leased by the government and renamed USS *Pert*, while Captain

Mayo's *Genesee Packet* was rechristened the *Hamilton*, all three vessels being part of Commodore Chauncey's fleet at Sackets Harbor. The *Growler* was abandoned by the Americans at French Creek (Clayton) when it went aground on a shoal as part of General Wilkinson's escort down the St. Lawrence in November 1813.

46. *New York Herald*, August 25, 1813.

47. Silvius Hoard had quite a career. He was hired by David Parish to supervise the building of the iron furnace at Rossie, he was a War of 1812 captain from St. Lawrence County, he was the postmaster at Antwerp from 1816 to 1818, he ran a tavern in Rochester in 1825 where Lafayette stayed on his tour of the United States and he wrote a letter to Henry Clay, secretary of state from Black Rock, New York, asking about settling at the mouth of the Columbia River. He died in Niagara Falls, New York, on September 23, 1828, and is buried in Ogdensburg Cemetery.

48. David Parish to Joseph Rosseel, February 17, 1813.

49. David Parish to Colonel Decius Wadsworth, March 11, 1813; David Parish to Commodore Chauncey, David Parish Letterbooks, vol. 4, 208 and 233.

50. David Parish to Joseph Rosseel, May 5, 1813, David Parish Letterbooks, vol. 4, 291.

51. In a letter to his brother David on August 4, 1813, Nathan Ford writes, "We expect Mr. Parish Sunday [August 8]." Also in that letter he writes, "I have advised Mr. Benbow to discontinue his operations so far or not to put the furnace into blast but have everything ready. I presume the British would not willingly have a furnace in their neighborhood making shot and shell to kill them with."

52. David Parish ledger book at the Ogdensburg Public Library, January 1811 entry; Nathan Ford to David Ford, July 9, 1814. Gilkison was well known in Ogdensburg and turns up in David Parish's ledger book as early as January 1811. Nathan Ford also mentions getting information from him concerning the British vessels building at Kingston in July 1814. In a letter to Isaac Todd of Montreal in August 1813, he refers to him as "my friend Mr. Gilkison in Prescott." David Parish Letterbook, vol. 4, 372.

53. Lieutenant Colonel Thomas Pearson to Sir George Prevost, August 9, 1813, Public Archives of Canada, RG 8 C Series 1A, 366–69 microfilm reel C-7173. The cipher used by Pearson is a simple alphabetic shift in which the letters of the original message are substituted with the letter seven places further down in the alphabet. For example, "A" in the original message is changed to "H," the eighth letter in the alphabet. Thus, the

cipher "WHYPZO" stands for "PARISH." The handwriting is quite difficult, and a few of the words in the original could not be made out.

54. David Parish to Colonel Thomas Pearson, August 10, 1813, Public Archives of Canada, RG 8 C Series 1A, vol. 14, 173–75 microfilm reel C-2610.
55. Colonel Thomas Pearson to David Parish, August 16, 1813, David Parish Papers in the National Archives of Canada.
56. George MacDonell to John Ross, September 13, 1813, Parish-Rosseel Collection. The letter ends with the British officer sending his "best respects" to Judge Ford, Captain Arnold and Mr. Parish.
57. John Ross to David Parish, April 2, 1814. This letter was translated by Professor Christine Zimmerman of St. Lawrence University. Ross states that the printing press is bound for Kingston, the temporary provincial capital, but it was ultimately bound for the new provincial parliament buildings then being constructed at York (now Toronto) to replace the ones burned by the Americans in April 1813. Kingston had been made temporary seat of the government of Upper Canada, and General Drummond mentions purchase of the press to the Parliament in April 1814. Drummond even notes that the press was obtained from Ogdensburg in his message to Lord Bathurst on April 12, 1814, stating that it is small and the type worn out but that it will suffice until a better one can be procured. See Kingsford, *History of Canada*, 439.
58. Stanley, *The War of 1812*, 5–6.
59. William Gilkison to Captain Robert Loring, April 7, 1814.
60. Gilbert Smissaert to David Parish, September 8, 1814.
61. John Ross to David Parish, December 14, 1814.
62. John Ross to David Parish, December 4, 1814.

Chapter 3

63. David Parish Ledger Book, Ogdensburg Public Library. The October 31, 1810 entry mentions Lieutenant Hicks. Joseph Rosseel wrote to David Parish on February 5, 1809, complaining of troops in Ogdensburg enforcing the embargo.
64. Joseph Rosseel to David Parish, April 25, 1809.
65. Joseph Rosseel to David Parish, March 21, 1809, and November 29, 1809.

66. The arsenal was situated just south of the village cemetery and one hundred feet or so off the main road. It was sold by the state in 1865 and later used as the village school. It partially burned in 1945, and the ruins were torn down later that year.
67. Note that both men, at this time, were militia generals, not U.S. Army generals.
68. Thomas Bridgum Benedict was born on October 23, 1783, in Woodbury, Connecticut, and married Mary Wilson on June 15, 1808. He was associated with Judge Cooper of Cooperstown, New York, and was in business with him in DeKalb. He rose from captain to brigadier general during the war. He moved to Ogdensburg with his wife and two children when commanding there and suffered a great financial loss at the capture of Ogdensburg in 1813.
69. Joseph Rosseel to David Parish, July 5, 1810.
70. Ibid. An advertisement in the February 19, 1811 *Ogdensburg Palladium* seeks out three journeymen rope makers for a year's work beginning April 1 and also invites bids to provide the lumber necessary for the three-hundred-foot-long building.
71. Joseph Rosseel to David Parish, May 22, 1812. Rosseel objected to the lease being transferred to Peter B. Porter, quartermaster general of the New York State Militia, until he agreed to pay $50 more per year for the loss of firewood on the property. Nathan Ford leased the old barracks to the U.S. government for $365 per year to be used by Forsyth's men (see his letter to General Dearborn on March 22, 1813). It is interesting to note that a fifteen-foot by seven-hundred-foot ropewalk was also converted to barracks at Sackets Harbor at about this time.
72. *Plattsburgh Republican*, August 7, 1812.
73. Ibid.; *Utica Patriot*, October 20, 1812. The latter article mentions Fort Rensselaer as being the principal fortification during the attack of October 4, 1812.
74. Bonney, *A Legacy of Historical Gleanings*, 198.
75. Malcomson, *A Very Brilliant Affair*, 71. Also in a letter from Van Rensselaer to Governor Tompkins, July 23, 1812, in Cruikshank, *Documentary History*, Part 1, 142. Hough claims that the operation was cancelled due to the movement of the ship to a different mooring location.
76. Nathan Ford to General Stephen Van Rensselaer, August 2, 1812.
77. Some sources state that the *Julia* escorted the commercial schooners up the river on September 5, 1812, piloted by Captain William Vaughn. This may be true, as a notice in the *Plattsburgh Republican* on September 18,

1812, reported that the British had sent over a message on September 3 informing the garrison at Ogdensburg that the armistice had expired and hostilities would commence in four days. The terms of the armistice required four days notice of hostilities.

78. *Commercial Advertiser*, August 15, 1812.

79. The flag in use on that day was the "Star Spangled Banner," with fifteen stars and fifteen stripes, as it had been for twenty years even though there were eighteen states in the Union at the time.

80. *Weekly Aurora*, September 1, 1812.

81. *Kingston Gazette*, September 26, 1812. Some of the information also comes from a report written by Forsyth and appearing in the October 30, 1812 edition of the *Plattsburgh Republican*.

82. *Utica Gazette* quoted in the *New York Herald*, October 7, 1812.

83. Morris, *Sword of the Border*, 30.

84. In *Sketches Illustrating the Early Settlement and History of Glengarry*, MacDonnell claims that it was about half that number of troops. Another source states that Lethbridge took with him 8 artillery men, 2 companies of the Canadian Fencibles, about 40 of the Newfoundland Regiment under Captain Robert P. Skinner and 150 Glengarry militia, who, after traveling the whole night, had arrived in carts from Cornwall, forty-eight miles away.

85. A British captain, Walker, was wounded and later applied for a year's pay in compensation for his wounds, but the British records failed to even record the ill-fated attack in their records, so he was denied a pension. (Canadian Archives Sessional Papers, vol. 32, issue 7, no. 8b, February 23,1822.) For some reason, Colonel Lethbridge was promoted to major general on June 4, 1813, although he had been passed over for an earlier promotion, with the opinion of his superiors being that he had held a frontier command but that his conduct "was so injudicious and so marked with deficiency in practical knowledge of his profession" that he was taken off the promotion list. (National Archives of Canada, RG 8, C-3526, vol. 1220, 169.

86. Swe-kat-si Chapter of the DAR, *Reminiscences of Ogdensburg*, 48. The October 6, 1812 account in the *Palladium* was reprinted in the Gettysburg *Centinel* on October 28, 1812. Church continued, "This is the way puppies get peoples' food: sneaking…there is always some puppy to run away with the credit." Note that Church mentioned in a letter to his son that he had exchanged fire with the British a total of seventeen times during the war and that the last time was the only one in which he gave ground. Only a few skirmishes are noted here because they are the only ones mentioned

in newspapers or other accounts. It would make sense that enemies so physically close to each other would be in conflict quite often.

87. Fredriksen, *Green Coats and Glory*, 30.

88. Ogdensburgh Palladium Nov. 10, 1812, quoted in the New York Herald Nov. 28, 1812 and Hough p. 628.

89. *New York Herald*, December 3, 1812; Louis Hasbrouck to his wife, November 20, 1812. The newspaper account states, "Mr. Parish very narrowly escaped being hit…just passed over his head when walking from the breastwork between the Red House and store. It struck just beyond him and bounded against Lyn's garden fence."

90. Louis Hasbrouck to his wife, November 20, 1812.

91. Benjamin Forsyth to the secretary of war, November 21, 1812, found in "Letters Received by the Adjutant General, 1812" at the National Archives, Washington, D.C.

92. *New York Herald*, December 15, 1812. The account in the *Herald* gives the date as November 26, 1812, whereas the *Plattsburgh Republican* of December 1, 1812 reports it as November 24.

93. Public Papers of Daniel D. Tompkins, 216.

94. Thomas Pearson to George Prevost, National Archives of Canada, RG 8 C-2936, vol. 387, 7–8.

95. Public Papers of Daniel D. Tompkins, 210.

96. Thomas B. Benedict to David Parish, February 2, 1813.

97. Strum, "The Politics of the New York Anti-War Campaign," 1–7.

98. "Elizabethtown" originally stood for a township and the village inside it. By 1812, there was a movement to rename the village after General Isaac Brock. By late 1812 or early 1813, after the death of General Brock, the village did become known as Brockville, which is what it is called today. At the time of Forsyth's raid, however, the village seems to have been called by either name. Most newspaper accounts of the time call it Elizabethtown, but Nathan Ford refers to it as Brockville in a letter to his brother dated February 13, 1813.

99. *Albany Argus*, February 16, 1813; *Northern Whig*, March 2, 1813. Both papers were quoting the Herkimer *American* of February 11, 1813.

100. *Northern Whig*, March 2, 1813, quoting the February 11, 1813 issue of the Herkimer *American*. It is not clear exactly who was in the jail at Brockville during the night of Forsyth's attack. The only thing certain is that they were either Americans or former Americans. McSween, the murderer not freed from the jail, had killed a fellow militia soldier who was trying to leave camp without permission. Bickham states that at his trial

later that year, McSween claimed the Americans offered him freedom but that he declined (see Leavitt and Bickham).

101. Joseph Rosseel to David Parish, February 6, 1813.

102. John Ross to David Parish, February 20, 1813.

103. George R. MacDonell (1780–1870) was a career officer, having joined the military at age sixteen. By the time of the Battle of Ogdensburg, he had risen to the rank of major but was temporarily given the local rank of lieutenant colonel to signify his seniority over other majors in theater whose date of rank may have preceded his. His name is spelled at least six different ways— McDonell, McDonnel, M'Donnell, MacDonald, etc.— in different accounts of the war. Harry F. Landon, editor of the *Watertown Daily Times* and accomplished historical writer, listed him as O'Donnell in his 1954 book *Bugles on the Border*. Note also that at least in the case of field-grade officers, regular army officers took precedence over militia officers in both the British and American forces.

104. John Ross to David Parish, January 23, 1813.

105. Joseph Rosseel to David Parish, February 12, 1813.

106. *Albany Argus*, February 2, 1813.

CHAPTER 4

107. Graves, *Fix Bayonets!*, 303–04.

108. Several streets have since been renamed. Euphemia Street became State Street, while Gertrude Street became Franklin Street.

109. The iron twelve-pound cannons of Kellogg's and Conkey's batteries were actually old British cannons that had been captured at Saratoga thirty-five years earlier.

110. Morris, *Morrises' History of Prescott*, 26-27.

111. *Kingston Gazette*, March 23, 1813.

112. Joseph Rosseel to David Parish, February 26, 1813.

113. Daniel W. Church to his son, December 9, 1850.

114. *Albany Argus*, March 5, 1813. The schooners and barracks were burned under the direction of Captain Thomas Fraser, who arrived after the battle but was detailed to supervise some of the destruction. Because he was not in the battle itself, he complained to the authorities that he was unfairly left off the list of those who should share in the prize money awarded to each participant.

115. Nathan Ford to David Ford, February 27, 1813.
116. The information concerning the Forsyth regimental records is found in the pension papers of Simon Powers at the National Archives in Washington, D.C. (Old War WF #17182).
117. Joseph Rosseel to David Parish, February 26, 1813; John Ross to David Parish, March 6, 1813.
118. Joseph Rosseel to an unnamed recipient in Albany, New York; reprinted in the March 12, 1813 *Albany Argus*.
119. Unsigned letter dated February 26, 1813, and printed in the March 15, 1813 edition of the *New York Evening Post*.
120. Louis Hasbrouck to his wife, April 9, 1813.
121. *New Hampshire Sentinel*, March 27, 1813.
122. John Ross to David Parish, March 6, 1813. Benedict tried to get the U.S. government to reimburse him for his financial losses at Ogdensburg, but the House of Representatives refused.
123. Joseph Rosseel to David Parish, March 5, 1813.
124. John Ross to David Parish, March 6, 1813.
125. *Ontario Repository*, June 1, 1813, quoting a May 12, 1813 letter from Ogdensburg.
126. "The fortress at Prescott is in the future to be called Fort Wellington." General Order, January 29, 1814, Public Archives of Canada, RG 8, vol. 1202 ½ J, 217. Microfilm C-3521.

CHAPTER 5

127. According to Nathan Ford in a letter to his brother dated April 10, 1813, Loring's cousin Charles Austin was killed by Thomas O. Selfridge in a famous incident in Boston on August 4, 1806. Selfridge had insulted the eighteen-year-old's father, and Austin caught him in State Street and beat him over the head with a heavy cane. Selfridge drew a pistol and shot Austin point-blank, killing him. He was tried for manslaughter and exonerated.
128. Hough, *A History of St. Lawrence and Franklin Counties*, 609.
129. Joseph Rosseel's Journal, 1807–1811.
130. David Parish to Joseph Rosseel, March 6, 1810.
131. *Ogdensburgh Palladium*, February 3, 1813.

132. Nathan Ford to David Ford, June 8, 1813.
133. Zebulon Pike Papers, Oneida County Historical Society.
134. The village of Massena was in the process of being renamed "Americus," but the name never really caught on. Marshall Massena, one of Napoleon's corps commanders, had fallen out of favor with the American people, and the locals were anxious to find their community another name. However, the renaming process seems to have been abandoned.
135. The men sent to Sackets Harbor were Elisha Dennison, Asa Day, Thomas Stedman, David Coffeen, John Phillips, Willard Seton, James Goddard and Uriel H. Orvis. George C. Conant had been the first postmaster when the Lisbon post office was established in 1809.
136. Loring Austin to Zebulon Pike, April 9, 1813.
137. Loring Austin to Zebulon Pike, April 10, 1813.
138. *Salem Gazette*, May 21, 1813.
139. The Fourth, Fifth and Sixth Amendments to the U.S. Constitution prohibit most of what the army did as far as arresting without proper warrants etc. However, the Eighth Amendment also prohibits the imposition of excessive bail, of which Judge Ford was guilty.
140. *Ogdensburgh Palladium*, April 21, 1813; quoted in the May 7, 1813 edition of the *New York Herald*.
141. Nathan Ford to David Ford, April 10, 1813.
142. *Albany Argus*, April 20, 1813.
143. Zebulon Pike to Nathan Williams, April 14, 1814. Williams was the district attorney for the Sixth District.
144. *Northern Whig*, April 20, 1813. The elections for New York State governor, lieutenant governor, senate and assembly were to be held in St. Lawrence County on Apr 27–29, 1813.
145. Zebulon Pike to Nathan Williams, April 14, 1813.
146. David Parish to Nathan Ford, April 28, 1813.
147. Louis Hasbrouck to his wife, April 9, 1813.
148. John Ross mentions in a May 27, 1813 letter to David Parish that Wells had been outside of the jail, whether as a free man or simply staying within the boundaries of the "jail limits" is unclear. Austin was back on active duty at Sackets Harbor by July 21 as a member of Captain Morgan's company of Light Dragoons.
149. Benjamin Raymond to Chief Justice James Kent, June 25, 1813. Raymond Collection.
150. Nathan Ford to David Ford, June 17, 1813.
151. Hough, *A History of St. Lawrence and Franklin Counties*, 383.

152. *New York Herald*, November 17, 1813.
153. Secretary of War John C. Calhoun to the Committee of Claims, January 2, 1818.
154. American State Papers, Class IX Claims, 1789–1823, 545.

Chapter 6

155. Reprinted in the June 2, 1813 *New York Herald.*
156. Louis Hasbrouck to his wife, May 14, 1813.
157. Graves, Fix Bayonets!, 297.
158. Due to contradicting dates and times in different sources, the details of Wilkinson's expedition were gleaned from several different sources and melded together in an effort to put it all into one logical sequence. The lion's share of credit must be given to Peter Graves's marvelous book *Field of Glory*, which formed the backbone of the narrative. Other sources used include Morris's *Sword of the Border*, Hough's *A History of St. Lawrence and Franklin Counties*, Alan Taylor's *The Civil War of 1812* and Lossing's *Pictorial Fieldbook of the War of 1812*.
159. Louis Hasbrouck to his wife, October 14, 1813. In a letter a month later, Hasbrouck insinuated that the only reason the dragoons were in Ogdensburg that day was to draw the cannon fire of the Prescott garrison. He claimed that the *Ogdensburgh Palladium* had satirized one of the American military leaders and that Colonel Luckett was sent for retaliation (see letter from Louis Hasbrouck to his wife, November 19, 1813). Luckett was raised from a marine lieutenant to a captain in the dragoons in February 1809 and then promoted to major on January 20, 1813, and to lieutenant colonel on August 1, 1813.
160. John Ross to David Parish, October 14, 1813. Nathan Ford was apparently the first to refer to Richards as "the Pope" in the spring of 1813, although he knew that Richards and his wife were Universalists and wrote that fact to his brother on March 16, 1813. He used "Pope" as a term of contempt.
161. Noah Freer to Lieutenant Colonel Thomas Pearson, October 20, 1813. National Archives of Canada, RG 8 C-3527, vol. 1221, 204. Major Cockburn's older brother George commanded the force that burned Washington, D.C., the following year.

162. Nathan Ford to David Ford, October 22, 1813; Hough, *A History of St. Lawrence and Franklin Counties*, 331.
163. Graves, *Field of Glory*, 82. Sherwood knew St. Lawrence County quite well and made several clandestine trips across the river for spying. As a matter of fact, it was Sherwood who informed Colonel Pearson in Prescott of the presence of Luckett's dragoons on October 16, leading to their capture.
164. Swift, *Memoirs of Gen. Joseph Gardner Swift*, 114–15. Swift mentions Arnold Smith of Morristown, who may have been the one to provide a plan of the fort at Prescott.
165. John Ross to David Parish, October 30, 1813.
166. Morris, *Sword of the Border*, 65.
167. Commodore Chauncey to General Wilkinson, November 4, 1813.
168. Lossing, *Pictorial Fieldbook*, 649.
169. Nathan Ford to David Ford, November 13, 1813.
170. The transcript of the letter appeared in the December 4, 1813 edition of the *New York Herald* and the January 15, 1814 *Kingston Gazette*. It also appeared in other Federalist papers in Albany, Utica and Philadelphia.
171. Ford's reference to "Golden Spurs" was aimed at recalling the public's attention to another one of Wilkinson's less than stellar performances. After Burgoyne's defeat in 1777, Wilkinson was tasked with carrying General Gates's messages to Congress. Wilkinson tarried on the way to see a girlfriend and arrived at the capital many days later than he should have. When a member of Congress proposed giving Wilkinson a golden sword, Representative John Witherspoon sarcastically suggested that golden spurs would have been more appropriate.
172. Note that although this letter from Ford appeared in several newspapers, there does not seem to be an independent source that can confirm whether or not Wilkinson ever said any such thing. Several people, including Dan Thorp, at whose house the tirade was supposed to have happened, later testified that they had seen and heard Wilkinson act strangely and profanely. Wilkinson vehemently denied it in his self-serving memoirs. In any event, Ford knew that Wilkinson's reputation as a scalawag would allow people to believe what they wanted. Major Birdsall, Owen Chatfield and Daniel Thorp all swore depositions in July 1819 detailing Wilkinson's drunken behavior while at Thorp's house. None of the three explicitly mention the ramblings that Ford alluded to. See Armstrong, *Notices of the War of 1812*, 211–12.
173. Nathan Ford to David Ford, November 13, 1813.

174. Public Archives of Canada, Q 127, no. 166, 428–31.
175. Gray was licensed to do so by the county in June 1809 at a house on Lot #46, "lately owned and occupied by Samuel Stacy." (q.v. in Chap. 7).
176. Kingston Gazette, November 6, 1813.
177. Cruikshank, *Documentary History*, Part 4. The name of the justice of the peaces appears as "Weegar" in some accounts but seems to be "Wager" in most records.
178. *New York Evening Post*, November 24, 1813.
179. Cook's Point and Crysler's Farm are both underwater today, but they were located on what is now the Ontario shore, nearly directly opposite from Wilson Hill on the New York side.
180. General Morgan Lewis wrote to his wife a few days later, "I have never suffered so much as I have done is this expedition."
181. Cruikshank, *Documentary History*, Part 8, 196.
182. National Archives of Canada, RG 8 Microfilm C-3173, vol. 681, 47.
183. Nathan Ford to David Ford, November 13, 1813.
184. George Prevost to Gordon Drummond, January 5, 1814. Public Archives of Canada, RG 8 "C" 678, 123.

CHAPTER 7

185. *Gouverneur Free Press*, January 8, 1913, 1. There is more information in the original.
186. Skeen, *Citizen Soldiers*, 98.
187. *Albany Gazette*, February 1, 1813.
188. *Northern Whig*, January 25, 1814.
189. In Canadian sources, this skirmish is often called the Battle of Matilda.
190. Up to 75 percent of Toussaint's Island was dredged away to form part of the main shipping channel for the Seaway in the late 1950s. A small sliver of the northern edge of the island is all that is now visible.
191. Croil, *Dundas*.
192. McComber had previously taught school at Buck's Bridge in the town of Potsdam, and his burial spot may now be underwater as a result of the flooding of the Seaway.
193. Major Rowland Heathcote to Colonel John Vincent, October 3, 1812. National Archives of Canada, RG 8 Microfilm C-3172, vol. 677, 147–49.

194. How a man named "Royal Tory" became a U.S. Army officer might be a story in itself. He lived in Columbia County, New York, in 1820.
195. National Archives of Canada, Microfilm RG 8 C-2647, vol. 89, 195–96.
196. Ibid., 198.
197. *Ontario Repository*, April 15, 1813.
198. Carter, *Story of Dundas*, 245.
199. National Archives of Canada, RG 8 C-3174, vol. 682, 222–23. Both of these affidavits are in the Canadian Archives with no explanation. The affidavits were dated December 13, 1813, and certified by Gouverneur Ogden, justice of the peace of Madrid.
200. Colonel John Harvey to Lieutenant Colonel John Walbach, November 14, 1813. National Archives of Canada, RG 8 C-3527, vol. 1225, 42-44. Colonel Harvey's use of the phrase "short continuance in this province" was just adding insult to injury.
201 Colonel John Walbach to Lieutenant Colonel Morrison, November 14, 1813. National Archives of Canada, RG 8 C-3233, vol. 691, 113–15.
202. Cruikshank, *Documentary History*, Part 9, 176–77. The source quoted is a general order from Edward Baynes, adjustant general in Quebec City, dated February 13, 1814.
203. Feltoe, *Redcoated Ploughboys*.
204. Hough, *A History of St. Lawrence and Franklin Counties*, 641–42.
205. National Archives of Canada, RG 8 C-3234, vol. 695, 115–20.
206. National Archives of Canada, RG 8 I C, vol. 682, 114.
207. As per British custom, each enlisted man was rewarded monetarily for his part in capturing the goods. The British army had a "prize master" who determined the value of the booty and then divided that amount of money among the troops. In this case, each private got thirteen shillings for the material captured at French Mills itself and an additional five shillings six pence for booty taken at Malone and Chateaugay between February 19 and 24. National Archives of Canada, RG 8 I C, vol. 1171, 276.
208. Hough gives the name as DeHeirne.
209. *Utica Patriot*, March 22, 1814, quoted in the April 19, 1814 *Ontario Repository*. This account is from a letter most likely written by Judge Hopkins himself.
210. Nathan Ford to David Ford, March 3, 1814.
211. Hough, *A History of St. Lawrence and Franklin Counties*, 314.
212. Public Archives of Canada, Upper Canada Sundries, 7405 and 7408.
213. Cruikshank, *A Study of Disaffection*.

BIBLIOGRAPHY

Books and Articles

Armstrong, John. *Notices of the War of 1812.* Vol. 2. New York: Wiley and Putnam, 1840.

Bickham, Tony. *The Weight of Vengeance: The United States, the British Empire and the War of 1812.* Oxford: Oxford University Press, 2012.

Bonney, Catharine Visscher. *A Legacy of Historical Gleanings*, Vol. 1. Albany, NY: J. Munsell, 1875.

Carter, J. Smyth. *The Story of Dundas: Being a History of the County of Dundas from 1784 to 1904.* Iroquois, ON: The St. Lawrence News Publishing House, 1905.

Croil, James. *Dundas; or, A Sketch of Canadian History.* Montreal: B. Dawson and Son, 1861.

Cruikshank, E.A. *The Documentary History of the Campaign upon the Niagara Frontier.* Welland, ON: Lundy's Lane Historical Society, 1905.

———. *A Study of Disaffection in Upper Canada in 1812–1815.* Ottawa, ON: Royal Society of Canada, 1912.

Feltoe, Richard. *The Call to Arms: The 1812 Invasions of Upper Canada*. Toronto, ON: Dundurn, 2012.

———. *Redcoated Ploughboys: The Volunteer Battalion of Incorporated Militia of Upper Canada, 1813–1815*. Toronto, ON: Dundurn, 2012.

Fredriksen, John C. *Green Coats and Glory: The United States Regiment of Riflemen, 1808–1821*. Youngstown, NY: Fort Niagara Publications, 2000.

Graves, Donald E. *Field of Glory: The Battle of Chrysler's Farm, 1813*. Toronto, ON: Robin Brass Studio, 2009.

———. *Fix Bayonets!: A Royal Welch Fusilier at War, 1796–1815*. Toronto, ON: Robin Brass Studio, 2007.

Hastings, Hugh, ed. *Public Papers of Daniel D. Tompkins, Governor of New York*. Albany, NY: J.B. Lyon Co. State Printers, 1898.

Hitsman, J. Mackay. "David Parish and the War of 1812." *Military Affairs* 26 (Winter 1962–63): 171–77.

Hough, Franklin B. *A History of St. Lawrence and Franklin Counties: From the Earliest Period to the Present Time*. Albany, NY: Little and Co., 1853.

Kingsford, William. *The History of Canada Under British Rule*. Toronto, ON: Roswell and Hutchison, 1892.

Landon, Harry F. "British Sympathizers in St. Lawrence County During the War of 1812." *New York History* 35 (1954): 131–38.

———. *Bugles on the Border: The Story of the War of 1812 in Northern New York*. Watertown, NY: *Watertown Daily Times*, 1954.

Leavitt, Thaddeus W.H. *The History of Leeds and Grenville Ontario*. Brockville, ON: Recorder Press, 1879.

Lossing, Benson J. *The Pictorial Fieldbook of the War of 1812*. New York: Harper and Brothers, 1869.

Macdonnell, John A. *Sketches Illustrating the Early Settlement and History of Glengarry in Canada*. Montreal: W. Foster, Brown and Co., 1893.

Malcomson, Robert. *A Very Brilliant Affair: The Battle of Queenstown Heights, 1812*. Kent, UK: Spellmount Publishers, 2004.

Morison, Samuel E. "The First National Nominating Convention, 1808." *The American Historical Review* 17 no. 4 (July 1912): 744–63.

Morris, John A.H. *Morrises' History of Prescott: 1800–2000*. Prescott, ON: St. Lawrence Printing Co., 2001.

Morris, John D. *Sword of the Border: Major General Jacob Jennings Brown, 1775–1828*. Kent, OH: Kent State University Press, 2000.

Skeen, Carl Edward. *Citizen Soldiers in the War of 1812*. Lexington: University Press of Kentucky, 1998.

Stanley, George F.G. *The War of 1812 Land Operations*. Canadian War Museum Historical Publication No. 18 Macmillan of Canada, 1983.

Strum, Harvey. "New York Federalists and Opposition to the War of 1812." *World Affairs* 142 no. 3 (Winter 1980): 169–87.

———. "The Politics of the New York Antiwar Campaign, 1812–1815." *Peace and Change* 8 no. 1 (April 1982).

———. "Property Qualifications and Voting Behavior in New York, 1807–1816." *Journal of the Early Republic* 1 no. 4 (Winter 1981).

———. "Smuggling in the War of 1812." *History Today* (August 1979): 532–37.

Swe-kat-si Chapter of the DAR. *Reminiscences of Ogdensburg*. Silver Burdett, NY, 1907.

Swift, Joseph G. *The Memoirs of Gen. Joseph Gardner Swift*. Privately printed, 1890.

Taylor, Alan. *The Civil War of 1812*. New York: Alfred A. Knopf, 2011.

Walters, Philip G., and Raymond Walters Jr. "The American Career of David Parish." *The Journal of Economic History* 4 no. 2 (November 1944): 149–66.

Primary Sources

Benjamin Raymond Papers, Potsdam (NY) Museum.

Daniel Church: Autobiographical Letters to His Son, 1850, Henry Sheldon Museum, Middlebury, VT.

Ford Family Fonds, Archives of Ontario, Toronto, ON.

Hasbrouck Collection, Ogdensburg (NY) Public Library.

Hopkins Collection, Ogdensburg (NY) Public Library.

Joseph Rosseel's Journal, 1807–1811, Parish-Rosseel Collection at the Owen D. Young Library Special Collections at St. Lawrence University, Canton, NY.

Loring Austin Letters, Mandeville Special Collections Library, University of California at San Diego.

Parish Ledger Book, Ogdensburg (NY) Public Library.

Parish Letter Books, New York Historical Society.

Parish-Rosseel Collection, St. Lawrence University, Owen D. Young Library Special Collections, Canton, NY.

Zebulon Pike Papers, Oneida County Historical Association, Utica, NY.

INDEX

J

K

L

M

N

O

P

R

S

T

V

W

Y

ABOUT THE AUTHOR

John Austin is a retired schoolteacher living in DeKalb, New York. He has researched and compiled lists of soliders from St. Lawrence County in both the Civil War and the War of 1812. He is a member of the St. Lawrence County Historical Society and enjoys using lesser-known resources for genealogical and historical research.